1979

CRIME
AND
SOCIETY

edited by ERIC OATMAN

THE REFERENCE SHELF
Volume 51   Number 2

THE H. W. WILSON COMPANY
New York   1979

THE REFERENCE SHELF

The books in this series contain reprints of articles, excerpts from books, and addresses on current issues and social trends in the United States and other countries. There are six separately bound numbers in each volume, all of which are generally published in the same calendar year. One number is a collection of recent speeches; each of the others is devoted to a single subject and gives background information and discussion from various points of view, concluding with a comprehensive bibliography. Books in the series may be purchased individually or on subscription.

Library of Congress Cataloging in Publication Data

Main entry under title:

Crime and society.

    (The Reference shelf ; v. 51, no. 2)
    Bibliography: p.
    1. Crime and criminals—United States—Addresses, essays, lectures.   2. Criminal justice, Administration of—United States—Addresses, essays, lectures.
I. Oatman, Eric F.   II. Series.
HV6789.C6883   364'.973   79-15089
ISBN 0-8242-0632-0

PRINTED IN THE UNITED STATES OF AMERICA

PREFACE

After a frightening seventeen-year rise, the rate of crime in the United States appears to be leveling off. Serious crimes—murder, rape, robbery, aggravated assault, burglary, larceny, and motor vehicle theft—rose an average of less than one percent from 1975 to 1976. From 1976 to 1977, the average rate of all 29 types of crimes that the FBI keeps track of dropped 3 percent. Preliminary figures for 1978 show a continued overall decline, especially in the North and in the East.

Though these figures may be reason for some relief, they give no cause for celebration. After all, since 1961, the rate of violent crimes has soared almost 200 percent. In the past five years, the overall rate of crime has risen 25 percent—eight times faster than the rate of population growth.

Moreover, the figures for 1977 are still shockingly high when translated into actual numbers of crimes: 19,000 murders, 63,000 rapes, 405,000 robberies—reports of 11 million serious crimes in all. Finally, the "dark shadow" of unreported crime—by some estimates as much as 35 percent of all robberies and 70 percent of all burglaries—adds a menacing dimension to all these statistics.

Clearly, crime is one of the nation's major problems. Its solution, if one exists, depends on the answers to a number of tough questions. Among them:

(1) What is the social and economic impact of crime on individuals and on American institutions?

(2) How well are American institutions—from families to prisons—coping with crime?

(3) Is crime an integral part of our social structure—springing, as former U.S. Attorney General Ramsey Clark has written, from "our national character and condition"?

The articles in this volume were selected to offer a re-

3

sponse to the last question, though in places they address all three questions. The issue of the social and cultural roots of crime is a central one, because we may be able to reduce crime by isolating and eliminating at least some of its causes. That those causes may prove elusive or ineradicable, or both, does not lessen the value of seeking answers. By learning more about the relationship of crime to American society, we learn more about ourselves—as a people, and as individual members of that society.

The articles have been organized into six sections. The first section looks at crime in several countries, including the United States, exploring in particular those attitudes, values, and societal changes that may promote or discourage criminal behavior. The next section reminds us that perceptions of crime have changed over the past two hundred years, that the definition of crime is elastic, and that keeping track of it is as much an art as a science, making the search for causes all the more difficult.

Section III examines white-collar and organized crime—two forms of crime that are deeply ingrained in our social institutions. The next two sections trace the search for the causes of crime over the past one hundred years, a period during which criminology matured as a discipline, drawing strength from the fields of medicine, psychology, and sociology. Finally, Section VI takes a look at society's response to crime—the criminal justice system.

"Crime is not the sort of problem that is amenable to breakthrough—as in health, with the Salk vaccine, or the technology that put a man on the moon," writes Gerald Caplan, a criminologist, in one of the selections in this compilation. It is the hope of the editor that this volume may help, in some small way, to point out the complexity of the problem of crime in America and to explain just why there are no simple solutions to the problem of crime in America, and why Americans should be suspicious of anyone who claims to have discovered one.

The editor would like to thank the various authors, publishers, and organizations who have granted permission for the use of materials in this volume.

ERIC F. OATMAN

May 1979

A NOTE TO THE READER

For further information, the reader's attention is directed to past Reference Shelf issues dealing with crime and criminal justice: *Crime and Its Prevention,* vol. 40, no. 4, published in 1968; *Justice in America,* vol. 44, no. 1, published in 1972; and *The Death Penalty,* vol. 49, no. 2, published in 1977.

CONTENTS

III. INSTITUTIONAL CRIME

IV. THE MAKING OF A CRIMINAL

V. YOUTH, POVERTY, AND RACE

VI. SOCIETY'S RESPONSE: CRIMINAL JUSTICE

I. VALUES, ATTITUDES, AND CHANGE

EDITOR'S INTRODUCTION

During a century of research and theorizing, criminologists have offered many conflicting explanations of the causes of crime. At first, the blame centered on the criminal's biological makeup. That theory (discussed in Section IV) has for the most part been discarded; today's high crime rate is more often attributed to a number of other interrelated factors, including individual personality, social structure, and culture. Weighing these factors, some observers say that the United States has the crime problem it deserves.

Yet nothing is quite so simple. We are told, on the one hand, that our congested cities, TV violence, and "soft" criminal sentences must share some of the blame. But those elements exist in modern Japan, too, where the murder and assault rates have been halved since 1955, and where the rate for robbery has been reduced by 90 percent over the past thirty years. David H. Bayley, the author of a study of police behavior in Japan and the United States, discusses these contrasts in the section's first article. From his observations, he draws a rather pessimistic moral for Americans.

In the second selection, "The Criminal Ethos," Ted Robert Gurr, a professor of political science at Northwestern University, notes that a rising crime rate is something the United States has shared with many other nations over the past twenty years. He blames a transformation in our mores —"a widespread weakening of the basic Judeo-Christian principle that thou shalt not steal or murder in the pursuit of private satisfactions."

Freda Adler, a professor of criminology and the author of the book *Sisters in Crime,* goes on to show how a change in cultural patterns can affect criminal behavior. More women are now suffering the same stresses and strains as men; they are committing more of the same crimes, too, and in similar ways.

"Society secretly *wants* crime," the psychoanalyst Karl Menninger once said. Law-abiding citizens, he felt, need criminals to "do for us the forbidden, illegal things we *wish* to do." In 1872, Jesse James and his gang held up the Kansas City *Star,* and a local newspaper hailed the act as "so diabolically daring and so utterly in contempt of fear that we are bound to admire it and revere its perpetrators."

The final selection—by Pete Hamill, a "hard-boiled" newspaper columnist for the New York *Daily News* and novelist—provides a glimpse at the ambivalent attitude Americans still have toward crime. In a piece that is all the more interesting because it appeared in a paper whose editorials are vehement in their defense of the forces of law and order, Hamill doffs his hat to the perpetrators of a recent exploit—the 1978 theft of more than $5 million from a New York airport.

CRIME IN JAPAN—LESSONS FOR THE U.S.[1]

Like the United States, Japan is modern, affluent, urbanized, and industrial. Politically and economically, Japan is part of the "developed" world. But there is one area where Japan is remarkably and perplexingly different—the incidence of criminality.

The number of crimes committed annually in Japan in recent years is actually lower than 25 years ago. . . . The crime rate—the incidence of crime per unit of population— is declining; in 1974, there were 112 crimes committed for every 10,000 persons. (This includes all penal code of-

[1] Article entitled "Learning About Crime—the Japanese Experience," by David H. Bayley, professor, author of *Forces of Order: Police Behavior in Japan and the United States.* Reprinted with permission of the author from *The Public Interest* No. 44 (Summer 1976), pp. 55–68. © 1976 by National Affairs, Inc.

fenses, no matter how trivial, except for traffic violations.)
Contrast this with the United States. . . . In 1974, including
only the seven categories of serious crime (murder, forcible
rape, robbery, aggravated assault, burglary, larceny-theft,
and auto theft) that the FBI uses to compute its crime index, there were 480 crimes for every 10,000 persons. In
other words, there are over four times as many serious
crimes per person in the United States as crimes of any sort
per person in Japan.

An individual is 10 times more likely to be murdered in
the United States than in Japan; 13 times more likely to be
raped; and six times more likely to be the victim of theft.
The most mind-boggling statistic concerns robbery, an offense that has a lot to do with the anxiety Americans feel
about "crime in the streets." The likelihood of being robbed
in the United States is *208 times* greater than in Japan.
Last year there were 436,000 robberies in the United States,
compared with 2,100 in Japan.

The difference between these figures is not due to statistical quirks. Robbery—theft accompanied by violence or the
threat of violence—is defined identically in the laws of both
countries. However, because possession of handguns is prohibited in Japan without official permission—which is given
only to the police, the armed forces, and the members of
international shooting teams—it is much less easy to intimi-
date, threaten, or coerce. While it is true that people kill,
not guns, as gun advocates in the United States assert, the
absence of guns nonetheless makes certain kinds of crime
more difficult to commit.

Comparison of crime rates in major urban areas in both
countries shows the same remarkable differences. There are
three times more serious crimes per person in New York
City than there are crimes of all sorts per person in Tokyo.
(So that New York City does not seem a particularly bad
American example, it should be noted that, according to
FBI statistics, there are at least 45 cities in the United States
with higher crime rates.) . . . .

Japan's low level of drug offenses represents a double

success—not just the achievement of a low incidence but the overcoming of what was once a large problem. During the mid-1950's and early 1960's, six times as many people were being charged with amphetamine offenses in Japan, and five times more with hard-drug offenses. . . .

Is the difference in criminality between Japan and the United States, shown by official figures, the result of misreporting? No. To be sure, more crimes are committed in both countries than are known to the police, but the rates of underreporting of crime, according to independent surveys in both countries, are the same or higher for the United States, depending on the type of crime. True crime in Japan is estimated to be about 80 per cent higher than what is reported, while true crime in the United States is 100 per cent higher. Official figures thus represent a real difference in criminality between the two countries.

The difference in public safety between Japan and the United States can be experienced and felt; it makes a difference in the way people live. Japanese streets and public places are habitable, even at night. . . .

American Theories of Crime

Why should there be this dramatic difference in criminality and public safety between these two wealthy, modern nations? Or what does the United States have that Japan doesn't? One place to look for explanations is among the theories that Americans produce to account for their own rising crime rate.

Crime is frequently attributed by Americans to social modernity. Rising crime rates are thought to be an inevitable consequence of modern industrial life. But there is not much to choose on this score between Japan and the United States. The economic structures of both countries are very similar: From a quarter to a third of the GNP of each country is produced by manufacturing, only three to six per cent by agriculture and fishing. Japanese agriculture is more labor-intensive than American, so more people work on farms than in the United States—17 per cent versus four per cent. This difference in occupational structure is too small to account for the disparity in national crime rates, and the difference between Japan and the United States is as great in urban crime rates as it is in rural crime rates.

Japanese as well as Americans are among the most highly educated people in the world. . . . Both populations are thoroughly exposed to mass media. Official estimates are that 95 per cent of all households in both countries have television sets; radios are even more common. . . .

Japanese are not quite as rich, however, as Americans. Though Japan is within the top 20 nations in the world in per capita income, ranking with Great Britain and Finland, per capita income is about 60 per cent of American levels—roughly $3000 versus $5000. This difference, though substantial, cannot account for the higher criminality in the United States. Few people would contend that affluence alone makes people criminal.

Americans often blame crime on urbanization, and especially population congestion. Newspapers have recently fed this line of speculation by reporting experiments showing that overcrowding among rats produces social deviance. Japanese experience refutes this explanation, unless one assumes that Americans and Japanese react very differently to crowding. The Japanese population is 10 times more densely concentrated than the American—about 110 persons per square mile, as opposed to nine per square mile. Though the proportion of people living in urban areas is the same in both countries—70 per cent—urban densities are significantly higher in Japan. . . . The United States would have a population density similar to Japan's if 50 per cent of all Americans lived in a space the size of the state of California.

Americans believe that the criminal justice system—police, prosecution, courts—bears a large responsibility for curbing the incidence of crime. When crime rates rise, the criminal justice system is thought to be failing. In recent years, inefficient policing and lenient sentencing have frequently been blamed. There would be less crime, it is argued, if there were more policemen, better trained and better equipped, so that more criminals were caught, and if sentences upon conviction were stricter, so that offenders spent more time behind bars. But if Japanese practices are a guide, Americans' expectations are misplaced. There are fewer policemen relative to the population in Japan than in the United States—one officer for every 563 persons versus one officer for every 410 persons. . . . On the other hand, because the territory of Japan is much smaller than the United States, Japanese policemen are more concentrated geographically—one officer for every 0.76 square miles in Japan as opposed to one for every 7.1 square miles in the United States. In Tokyo there are 182 policemen per square mile, in New York City only 51. If, therefore, changes in police coverage can affect the crime rate, the crucial ratio would seem to be between policemen and area, not between policemen and population. . . . Proportionately, the Japanese spend more of their national wealth on policing than Americans do—0.80 per cent of GNP in Japan, 0.56 per cent in the United States. Relative to Japan, then, the United States could afford to increase police personnel in order to lower the policeman/territory ratio. One might speculate that this might, following the Japanese model, reduce crime somewhat.

Contrary to what might be expected, court sentences are not more severe in Japan than in the United States. In recent years about 96.5 per cent of Japanese convicted of crimes were sentenced to payment of a fine, and only 3.5 per cent were sentenced to imprisonment. Moreover, a majority of those sentenced to prison were given a suspended sentence. Though experts agree that these sentences are much more lenient than in the United States, the point is not easy to substantiate statistically. . . . Comparing penal sentences for the few crimes common to United States and Japanese criminal codes, the average sentence for counterfeiting is 40 months in the United States, 15 months in Japan; for forging public documents, 31 months in the United States, 11 months in Japan. Stricter sentences are also not the explanation for the dramatically lower rate of narcotics offenses in Japan. Sentences for offenses involving hard drugs in Japan average two years, as opposed to between five and six years in the United States. Japanese law does provide for compulsory hospitalization, and the practice is to take addicts off drugs immediately, to go "cold turkey." The death penalty does exist in Japan, and is most commonly given for murder attendant upon robbery. During the period 1968 through 1972, 68 persons were executed —about 13 per year.

In the late 1960's, burning cities and the findings of a national commission prompted Americans to discover violent national traditions generally unacknowledged in history books. Finding that violence was "as American as apple pie," as Rap Brown said, Americans began to blame the past for contemporary criminality. Unfortunately for this line of argument, traditions of violence are by no means unique to the United States. Japan has them as well. Student demonstrations, for example, more sustained and more violent than the antiwar movement in the United States, have been a fixture of Japanese politics for a generation. Assassination of political figures has a much larger place in Japanese history than in American history. . . .

Japanese television is as inundated with bloody samurai dramas as American television has been with shoot-outs at the OK corral. If America has a cult of the gun, Japan has a cult of the sword. Japanese history is no less blood-soaked or cruel than American history. It would be difficult to argue that contemporary Japanese culture bears fewer traces of its own past than American culture does of its own past.

Informal Social Controls

So where do we turn if modernity, congestion, the criminal justice system, or violent traditions do not explain the difference in crime rates? An alternative approach is to free ourselves from American views about the causes of crime and examine what Japanese society does to control deviance that Americans do not customarily consider. Rather than measuring Japanese criminality against American theories, let us consider it against the perspective of Japanese practice.

The key to social discipline in Japan lies in the greater vitality of informal controls over individuals. Japan relies less than the United States on formal institutions of government—such as police, prosecutors, and courts—to curb criminality. Order is maintained through active informal supervision of personal behavior by family, workmates, and neighbors. This informal system has three interlocking features that contrast sharply with American social practices: the vitality of informal groups, the legitimacy of authority, and the assumption by informal groups of responsibility for maintaining social order.

Despite industrialization and urbanization, Japan has preserved the cohesion of small-scale social groups more successfully than the United States. Personal identity for Japanese, who prize mobility and individual autonomy less than Americans do, is dependent on membership in particular groups. Social position is defined more idiosyncratically than in the United States. A Japanese is not just an engineer, but an engineer with Mitsubishi, educated at Tokyo University; not simply a civil servant, but a civil servant in the Accounting Section of the Ministry of Finance with 15 years seniority; not simply a brother, but a brother in the Matsuoka family of the Setagaya ward of Tokyo, formerly of Kurashiki in the Okayama Prefecture; not simply a police officer, but an Inspector in the Crime Prevention Section of the Shibuya Police Station. While in the United States people are also known by their associates, in Japan they are almost unrecognizable without these affiliations. This explains why personal introductions and name cards specifying social location are so crucial in Japan. They ensure that the newcomer is affiliated with, and hence responsible to, people who are known and trusted. The American cocktail party makes Japanese acutely uncomfortable because it forces them to interact with anonymous, essentially interchangeable people.

Because of their dependence on particular groups, Japanese are extremely sensitive to the regard of these associates. They shrink from any action that might jeopardize their acceptability, for the greatest calamity that could befall them would be exclusion. Then they would be outcasts, eternal strangers without the emotional fulfillment of belonging. As a result, Japanese have, in the apt phrase of one commentator, a "heightened sense of the fatefulness of their antisocial impulses." Americans, by contrast, value social mobility; they want to be able to pull up stakes, to sever dependency, to be autonomous. . . . Japanese live within stable networks of named people; Americans live in a more impersonal human environment, where people are substitutable. Social constraints in Japan are thus less diffuse than in the United States; they are overlaid with the emotions of personal attachment.

The capacity for exerting the kind of social control found in Japan has been eroded in the United States. For example, a larger proportion of families remain intact in Japan than in the United States. . . . Americans are probably the most mobile people in the world, and this has a direct effect on the cohesiveness of families and neighborhoods. . . .

Neighborhoods are also more cohesive in Japan. For example, most have institutions of informal government, known as *chokai,* that collect dues, elect officers, undertake projects, and disseminate information. The *chokai* are not creations of law but rather traditional institutions, centuries old. Similar organizations have been lost in most places in the United States and must now be reinvented, often as a direct response to soaring crime and a need for greater security.

There is, then, a structural difference between Japanese and American society that is critically important to the incidence of crime. Japanese are surrounded by tight networks of known individuals to whom they are connected by blood or shared experience, and whose regard is essential for emotional security. This produces a capacity for in-

formal constraint of behavior that is very much stronger
in Japan than in the United States.

The Legitimacy of Authority

The Japanese also more readily accept the legitimacy
of such informal authority. The characteristic posture of a
Japanese before authority is subservience and compliance;
the characteristic posture of an American is self-assertion
and suspicion, often resentment. . . . Guilty pleas in court
are more common in Japan than in the United States—95
per cent versus 80 per cent of all prosecutions. Moreover,
many of the American guilty pleas are technical—the
result of plea-bargaining—and do not indicate repentance
or admission of error. Plea-bargaining is illegal in Japan.
The compliant nature of Japanese offenders is shown by an
amazing fact: 90 per cent of all Japanese criminal cases are
prosecuted without the necessity of jailing an offender to
guarantee his court appearance. At no time from detection
through trial is the offender detained. . . .

Confronted by authority, Americans struggle and conform; Japanese submit and repent. Admissions of guilt and
a display of contrition are conditions for reacceptance of
an offender into Japanese society. They indicate that the
individual recognizes and acknowledges his transgression
against the standards of the community; resocialization has
begun. Though contrition is also rewarded in the United
States, it is not required for reacceptance. All that is necessary is for the offender to meet the requirements of punishment—to pay his debt, to serve his time.

The efficiency of these two criminal justice systems is
sharply affected by the customary responses of the people
to authority. Suspects are found by the Japanese police in
connection with 57 per cent of all known offenses, while
the comparable figure in the United States is a bare 20 per
cent. . . . Since admissions of guilt occur in 95 per cent
of prosecutions in Japan, and 80 per cent in the United
States, conviction is assured with respect to 35 per cent
of known offenses in Japan, against 13 per cent in the

United States. By the yardstick of convictions, the Japanese criminal justice system is almost three times more effective than the American.

To the extent that the Japanese criminal justice system deters crime, it does so not because it is severe, but because it is certain. The chances of escaping exposure and censure are much less in Japan than in the United States. The cornerstone of the American philosophy of crime control is deterrence: People will not commit crimes if punishment is prompt and strict. Official action is supposed to reinforce the development of conscience, the internalization of moral restraint. Japanese experience suggests that the relationship between formal action of a criminal justice system and the incidence of crime is more complex. Rather than official action prompting compliance with social norms, compliant attitudes toward authority enhance the efficiency of official action. The Japanese police look good because the offender will admit guilt in order to obtain social acceptance. Because authority is informally present throughout society and people accept its legitimacy, criminal justice officials in Japan have a comparatively easier time detecting and prosecuting offenders than their counterparts in the United States. There is a disturbing implication in this for the United States: Once the volume of crime becomes very large, and the system becomes overloaded—as one can argue has already happened in the United States—then both the efficiency of law-enforcement and its deterrent effect decline. Because official efficiency and the volume of crime are reciprocally related, a spiral of increasing crime and decreasing efficiency would be difficult to reverse. Formal systems of control work best when they are needed least. Unfortunately, the converse is also true.

Law and Morality

The last feature in the Japanese system of crime control that needs stressing is the permeability of the boundary between formal and informal authority. Police, prosecutors, and courts possess not merely legal authority, as in the United States, but moral authority as well. Japanese police officers sermonize considerably more often than American officers: They lecture people of all ages and stations on the obligations of being a "proper Japanese," on manners, on courtesies appropriate to elders, on the danger of bad companions, and on the obligations of friendship. Americans tend to separate moral and legal authority, assigning them to different persons—legal authority to policemen, moral authority to priests, teachers, and relatives. They resent the assumption by either set of the other's role. A moral figure that helps the police is a "fink"; a legal figure that sermonizes is told to make a formal charge or else "bug off."

Formal and informal roles, legal and moral ones, interpenetrate in Japan because government is not considered a created entity—it is not the result of an explicit act of fabrication by an existing community, the product of making a constitution. Government is not added on to community; it is intrinsic to community, as parentage is to family. Its role is larger than law, and consequently more difficult to circumscribe. Government officials, such as policemen, have a legitimacy, a moral stature, that they do not have in the United States. They are agents of the community's moral consensus as well as its statutory prescriptions.

The homogeneity of the Japanese population has undoubtedly been important in allowing community and government, morality and law, informal and formal authority, to become combined. Because subcultural groups are few and their numbers very small, there is almost universal agreement on what it means to be Japanese, as well as the value of being so. . . . Altogether, less than three per cent of the population have minority status, and the majority of these are solidly Japanese in appearance and culture. While the melting pot of American society is still bubbling and giving off smoke and fumes, Japanese society has produced an ingot of uniform quality.

As Japanese policemen are accepted as moral actors, Japanese citizens are expected to assist policemen actively.

The responsibility for maintaining law and order does not belong exclusively to police, prosecutors, and judges. The roles of private citizen and public official mutually interpenetrate. For example, almost every neighborhood in Japan has a crime prevention association composed of citizen volunteers and led by their own officials. These associations, working closely with local police stations, distribute material on household security, warn residents about new forms of crime, post reminders in public places about the importance of telephoning the police promptly if any suspicious events occur, maintain half a million "contact points" in private homes where crime-prevention information may be obtained, and sell special locks and fasteners for doors and windows. In many neighborhoods the associations organize street patrols, some with distinctive uniforms, that give special attention to monitoring the behavior of juveniles during the evening hours in popular entertainment areas. Officers in each police station are designated to work with the associations. . . .

Americans, on the other hand, are unsure of their relations with the police when they are not charged with an offense. Though recognizing that they have a duty to cooperate with the police, they interpret this narrowly, and have devised no mechanisms for giving assistance to the police in an organized, reliable, routine way. Though vigorously defending the right of self-defense, Americans believe that policing should be left to formal authorities. They are suspicious of individuals who go out of their way to lend assistance. Group assistance especially has a bad reputation, having become associated in American history with vigilantism. . . .

In summary, the fundamental reason why Japan has a crime rate that is significantly lower than the United States is because its people are encapsulated by familiar small-scale groups that articulate norms of right behavior—norms that are similar from group to group—and apply informal pressure to conform. Economic growth, industrialization, and technological modernization have not produced social atomization in Japan. Though Japan has experienced the same great economic changes as the United States during the past century, its society remains vitally cellular. The economic and social basis for grouping has changed, but the subordination of individuals to groups with responsibility for them remains. Japan is unique among industrial societies in its ability to create and maintain tribe-like groups of small scale. This is fundamental to maintaining low levels of criminality.

The small size of Japan also makes some contribution to its relative peaceableness, but it is unclear how much. . . .

The Future of the American System

Two final observations about crime and law enforcement in the United States are prompted by this examination of the Japanese experience. First, the levels of criminal behavior that Americans find so disturbing may be the inevitable consequence of aspects of national life that Americans prize—individualism, mobility, privacy, autonomy, suspicion of authority, and separation between public and private roles, between government and community. The United States may have relatively high levels of criminality because it is inhabited by Americans.

Second, given American traditions, it is questionable whether law enforcement agencies can be much more effective in curbing criminality than they are now. The record so far would indicate that government, unless supported by more vigorous informal social sanctions, cannot contain crime without running the risk of transforming the scope and character of its operations in ways that would threaten other values basic to the American way of life. Moreover, reliance on formal agencies of the criminal justice system may be more than merely ineffective—it may undermine their public support. It is more than a coincidence that rising concern with crime in the United States is accompanied by fierce criticism of the criminal justice system. Though different people have their particular scapegoats, most would agree that the "system" is not

working well. Of course it is not: It is being asked to do
what it cannot do—namely, take the place of decaying
processes of informal social control. Americans are in the
tragic and paradoxical position of depending more and
more on law-enforcement institutions whose authority they
increasingly question and reject.

THE CRIMINAL ETHOS[2]

In the eighteen-twenties London was Europe's largest
city, the commercial and political hub of the world's most
prosperous society and greatest empire. It was also a
dangerous, crime-ridden place. Professional robbers and
receivers flourished in neighborhoods where it was worth
a prosperous man's life and possessions to venture at night.
Thousands of street urchins lived by petty theft during the
day and slept in the noisome alleyways and courtyards. A
contemporary writer summed up London's squalor and
disorder when he denounced the city as "the infernal wen."
The criminal laws designed to control the rampant
crime of Georgian England had a harsh bite. The death
penalty was specified for more than two hundred offenses,
on the widely accepted principle that severe punishment
was an effective deterrent. But no centralized, professional
police force existed to catch offenders. Constables, professional "thief-takers," and private citizens hailed petty offenders before magistrates who seldom were trained in law
and were often venal and corrupt. The judges who heard
serious cases had neither the legal discretion nor the in-
clination to be lenient. The defendant's hopes rested with
the reluctance of many a jury to convict in capital cases, or
the mercy of the Crown in commuting his death sentence to
transportation to the Australian penal colonies. Such pris-

[2] From article by Ted Robert Gurr, author, Payson S. Wild Professor of
Political Science at Northwestern University, co-director (1968–69) of the National Commission on the Causes and Prevention of Violence. *The Center Magazine.* 11:74–79. Ja. '78. Reprinted with permission of the *Center* Magazine, a
publication of the Center for the Study of Democratic Institutions, Santa Barbara,
California.

ons as existed aimed neither to punish nor rehabilitate. Jails held debtors and those waiting to be tried or executed; the bridewells [houses of correction] put vagrants and other petty offenders to forced labor for the profit of their officials.

Between the eighteen-twenties and the eighteen-seventies this hodgepodge was transformed into a modern system of criminal justice. A series of parliamentary acts overhauled the criminal law, penalties were prescribed in proportion to the seriousness of the offense, the death penalty was abolished for all but the most heinous crimes. London's patchwork police services of river police and Bow Street runners, constables and parish watchmen, were replaced in 1829 by the centralized Metropolitan Police. The courts were improved. Beginning in the eighteen-fifties child thieves were committed to new reformatories and kept there long enough to receive basic education and work training. Adult offenders were sentenced to long terms in the new convict prisons, where discipline was harsh and rehabilitation piously sought through hard, monotonous labor.

The zeal of London's new "bobbies" showed up at first in increased arrests and convictions. But by the eighteen-fifties common crime seemed on the decline and by the end of Queen Victoria's reign the city was thought by the English and visiting continentals alike to be one of the most orderly in all Europe. The official statistics suggest to social historians that the trend continued to the late nineteen-twenties, when the conviction rate for all indictable (serious) offenses was one-ninth of the eighteen-forties level. Police statistics on known offenses and arrests, first published in 1869, are especially convincing. Known serious offenses fell by an average of ten per cent per decade for sixty years thereafter. The arrest rate for all offenses, serious and petty ones, was down by a ratio of three to one despite a steady increase in the absolute and proportional size of the Metropolitan Police Force. Data on convictions show assault down by a ratio of five to one, total theft by four to one, robbery by more than ten to one. Burglary was the only serious offense to go against the trend, thanks to the activities of a small cadre of professional housebreakers who became increasingly successful at eluding the police.

The history of successful crime control in nineteenth- and early-twentieth-century London has many parallels. All England and Wales experienced improvements in proportion to those of the metropolis. In Sydney, Australia, at literally the opposite end of the earth, officials followed England's lead in reforming criminal justice, and indicators of convictions fell by ratios of ten to one and more. In Stockholm—a far smaller city in a very different society—high crime and the reforming impulse also coincided in the second quarter of the nineteenth century. The results were much the same. In the century between the eighteen-forties and the nineteen-thirties the rate of convictions for crimes against persons in Stockholm declined by a ratio of about four to one and thefts by five to one. American studies identify similar trends in the annals of common crime in cities as varied as Boston, Salem, and Chicago.

We lack enough historical evidence to be certain that the century of improvement in public order was a universal Western experience. Widespread it certainly was, and it contributed to an abiding faith in the efficiency of the criminal justice policies which seemed to have produced it. But the story does not have a happy ending, because every one of the cities and countries just mentioned is today experiencing a runaway increase in rates of common crime. And the paradox is that the institutions and policies of criminal justice which have failed to stem the contemporary resurgence of disorder are essentially the same as those which helped reduce crime to its low ebb in the early decades of this century.

The common Western experience of rising crime is worth documenting, if only to help dispel the notion that America's contemporary social problems, along with her tattered virtues, are somehow unique. In London, rates of common crime started upward in the depth of the Depression. They subsided after World War II, but in the

early nineteen-fifties began an inexorable increase. Indictable offenses known to police grew by 450 per cent between
1950 and 1974, with the nastiest kinds of crimes increasing
most sharply; burglaries are up five hundred per cent, rape
by six hundred per cent, assault by nine hundred per cent,
and robbery by 1,200 per cent. London has been the bell-
wether for all England and Wales, whose rate of murder
and assault combined grew by nine hundred per cent between 1950 and 1974, and burglary and robbery combined
by five hundred per cent.

London's experience is paralleled throughout the English-speaking world (see Table 1, page 29). The late
nineteen-forties and early nineteen-fifties marked the low
ebb of common crime in virtually every English-speaking
country. Since then the trends have been consistently upward. In the United States, homicides and assaults together
have increased at an average of nineteen per cent per year
for a generation. Elsewhere the nineteen-fifties rates for
murder and assault were lower but the increases have been
swifter. The rising trends in theft have been sustained just
as long, and average between eight and fourteen per cent
per annum. The most serious forms of property crime—
robbery and burglary—have risen about twice as rapidly as
total theft in all these societies. Ireland seems the most
favored country in this comparison. Its relatively low volume of crime may be credited to its Gaelic culture, religious traditionalism, or simply the smallness of its cities.
But these conditions have not inhibited the Irish from
emulating the growing Anglo-American fondness for may-
hem and theft.

Explanations abound for rising crime in these countries.
Substantial social and economic inequalities exist in all of
them. Everywhere the penal system is excoriated because
it warehouses offenders rather than rehabilitating them.
The police often are accused of corruption and a heavy-
handed disregard for civil liberties. Add to this the special
explanations proffered by social analysts confronted with
rising crime in particular countries. Britain? Class tensions

TABLE 1
Crime Trends in English-Speaking Societies
Known Murders and Assaults
per 100,000 Population

	1950	c. 1960	1970's*	Average annual increase
England and Wales	13.0	32.4	127.8	37%
London	13.0	26.2	123.5	35%
United States	58.0	91.2	225.1	12%
New South Wales	no data	15.5	21.7	4%
Canada	no data	158.2	419.1	15%
Republic of Ireland	5.9	13.7	29.6	19%

Known Thefts per 100,000 Population

	1950	c. 1960	1970's*	Average annual increase
England and Wales	847	1,317	2,454	8%
London	1,056	1,942	3,624	10%
United States	1,108	1,786	4,588	13%
New South Wales	no data	604	1,467	14%
Canada	no data	1,408	3,443*	13%
Republic of Ireland	346	472	1,090	10%

* Data from 1974 except New South Wales (1970), Ireland (1971), and Canada (1973).

in a declining economy. The United States? An angry black underclass, its hopes stirred by promises of a Great Society which never arrived. Ireland? Modernization is eroding traditional acceptance of poverty and authority. Australia? Merely beery, exuberant youths challenging unpopular police.

If there is any universal truth to these kinds of conventional liberal wisdom about the social origins of crime, the Scandinavian countries surely should be more favored than some of the English-speaking nations. They are ethnically homogenous and their social ethos is strongly egalitarian. Their cities are free of slums and their social services are among the best in the world. Economically they have prospered since the end of World War II and have had low unemployment. Their police are widely respected, justice is ordinarily even-handed and efficient. Rehabilitation is the central, overriding aim of their penal system.

Stockholm provides a historical laboratory for observing crime in Scandinavia. Unlike London, the Great Depression of the nineteen-thirties had little effect on its crime rates. During wartime, crime in neutral Stockholm rose and then subsided—until about 1950. Since then virtually every category of offense against persons and property has skyrocketed. These are some twenty-year increases in crimes known to police: murder and attempts, six hundred per cent; assault and battery, more than three hundred per cent; rape and attempted rape, three hundred per cent; "crimes inflicting damage" (i.e., vandalism), five hundred per cent; all theft, three hundred and fifty per cent; robberies alone, one thousand per cent; fraud and embezzlement, seven hundred per cent. In 1971, there was one theft reported to police for every eleven inhabitants of the city, which can be compared with 1974 figures of one per twenty Londoners, and one per eighteen New Yorkers. In fairness to Stockholmers, they are more likely to report thefts to their trusted police than are cynical New Yorkers. The point remains that Swedish welfare and criminal justice policies have not inhibited the rise of urban crime.

Stockholm represents in most severe form a criminal malaise that has affected all of Scandinavia. . . . On the face of it the Scandinavian countries have higher rates of common crime than most of the English-speaking countries. Not too much should be made of the differences, since national crime-accounting systems vary. Trends within each country are more reliably assessed than absolute differences among them.

In the heartland of Western Europe the portrait of crime is significantly different in one major respect. There are no long-term increases in murder and assault in the continental democracies. Congratulations are premature, though, since Germany and France both began to move up in the late nineteen-sixties. . . .

From the Marxist-Leninist point of view, this evidence of the rising tide of disorder in Western societies is the harbinger of capitalism's long-awaited collapse. The Eastern European commentators who offer this interpretation no doubt are uncomfortably aware that their own societies are suffering a similar affliction. . . .

There is finally the case of Japan, an industrialized democratic society which has had unparalleled success in reducing crime rates—serious crime most of all—during the last two decades. . . .

This pattern of change duplicates what happened in London, Stockholm, and Sydney during their century of falling crime: as public order improved, serious offenses declined more rapidly than petty ones. And it is the reverse of what is happening in contemporary Western societies in which serious property crime has increased far faster than petty offenses.

These contrasts and images imply that a fairly high level of petty theft is endemic to prosperous societies, but that serious crime is not. Japan is a case in point. It is a capitalistic society which has had extraordinary success in reducing the incidence of murder, assault, and robbery. The improvement has been a sustained one—some twenty-five years in duration—and it has taken place in a society undergoing the rapid social and economic changes that elsewhere are assumed to be crimogenic.

In the face of nineteenth- and twentieth-century examples of successful social defense, it is reasonable to ask where contemporary Western societies have gone wrong.

We can begin to clear the ground of some incorrect or partial explanations, and perhaps point out where the most general answers are to be found.

In pop sociology it has been fashionable to blame rising crime rates on intensified policing and more thorough crime-reporting systems. Contemporary examples of both can be found: there are wide fluctuations in police attention to "victimless" crimes like prostitution and drug abuse, while changes in reporting systems produce abrupt discontinuities in crime statistics. But neither explanation accounts for persistent trends up or down in the rate of common crime.

The "better policing" explanation of rising rates of common crime is largely a myth. It is naive to think that crime statistics depict precisely the real incidence of crime because many victims, especially in high-crime areas, think it is useless to report their losses. But there is little doubt that the long-term trends common to postwar Western societies reflect real changes in social behavior of large magnitude. This is the social issue most in need of explanation, not the vagaries of police behavior.

The typical robber or thief in Western societies—past and present—is all too likely to be a poor, uneducated denizen of an urban slum. The liberal view has long been that common crime should therefore be reduced by social and economic improvement. The nineteenth-century experience of cities like London and Stockholm provided much sustenance for that belief. The late-twentieth-century experience has badly undercut it. Literacy and free schooling through the secondary level are universals in Western society. Supportive social services are far better now than in 1920 or 1950. The conditions of urban life, including housing quality, have improved throughout the twentieth century and especially since 1945; the United States is the only Western society whose urban environment has worsened appreciably in the last thirty years.

In economic terms more people live better than ever before. Inevitably some are poorer than others and some are unemployed, but a net of public support catches virtually all of them before they reach the margin of subsistence. The sophisticated liberal explanation for rising crime in prospering societies is no longer misery but resentment over one's "relative deprivation" at being left behind while almost everyone else seems to be getting richer. Theft then becomes an easy, albeit illicit, way to close the gap. And one basic reason theft in modern societies is easy is that there is so much more to steal than there was half a century ago.

These "relative deprivation" and "opportunity" explanations of rising theft are plausible but not proven, and in any case partial. They do not account for the equally sharp rise in crimes against persons. More fundamentally, they do not explain why the hypothetical victim of deprivation chooses the risks of crime over the manifold legitimate opportunities for personal advancement. The answer to this question lies less in the social environment than in people's beliefs about how they *should* respond to its variegated opportunities. In other words, it is a question of norms and morality. The rising frequency of common crime is prima-facie evidence of a widespread weakening of the basic Judeo-Christian principle that thou shall not steal or murder in the pursuit of private satisfactions.

The supposition that value change lies at the bottom of the "crime problem" is reinforced by evidence about the explosion of youth crime. . . .

The supposition is that youth crime is high because the family, schools, and churches have failed to implant traditional values. It is problematic whether the socializing institutions really do worse than in the past because there is no direct evidence on whether they were more uniformly effective at the turn of the century, or in the nineteen-twenties and nineteen-thirties. But there is no doubt that contemporary youths have an alternative to traditional teachings. Distinctive new "post-industrial" values were articulated on university campuses during the nineteen-sixties and soon echoed by young people throughout Western society. The counter-culture's creed had many elements that were consistent with traditional values. It had other elements, encapsulated in the slogan, "Do your own thing," which are socially more corrosive and seem to have attracted wider and more enduring support than its humanitarian abstractions.

The most corrosive form of this alternative ethic is aggressive hedonism, a belief that almost any means are justified in pursuit of personal aggrandizement. It appears to be a mutation of Western materialism, stripped of its work ethic and generalized from material satisfactions to social and sexual ones. Moreover it often coexists with a sense of resentment against large, impersonal organizations —more because of their remoteness and unresponsiveness than because of tangible failures in performance. This alienation—to give it the proper sociological label—is manifest in the decline of authority of state and corporation, school and church, and in a growing defiance of their rules.

The proposition is that a distinctive syndrome of selfishness and alienation has taken root in the interstices of most Western societies. It is especially prevalent among youth, though it is not unique to them; and one of its manifestations is the rise in youthful aggression and theft that accounts for most of the rise in Western crime rates. This hypothesis is not easily tested, nor does it point toward any simple social cures, except in one ironic sense. The invisible hand of hedonism has dictated that an unprecedentedly large proportion of young people in Western societies forgo having the children who would become the potential criminals and victims of the nineteen-nineties.

One thing this tentative explanation does help us understand is why the criminal law, police, courts, and prisons together cannot restrain the rising tide of crime. These institutions and their policies were effective in turn-of-the-century societies dominated by a self-confident middle class convinced that prosperity in this life and salvation in the next could be achieved through piety, honesty, and hard work. All authorities spoke with the same voice. The institutions of public order were effective because they reinforced the dominant view. They did not merely punish those who transgressed. They were missionaries to the underclass, informing them of the moral order through arrest, trial, and imprisonment.

Today, no self-confident consensus on standards of behavior is to be found in Western societies. There are many self-proclaimed authorities offering many alternatives. Bereft of a solid foundation of social support, the police, courts, and prisons drift.

THE RISE OF THE FEMALE CROOK[3]

Even though female emancipation in America is still young we have already become accustomed to the female traffic cop, the female bank executive, the female airline pilot, and the female telephone lineman. But suddenly we are faced with the fact that there are female car thieves, muggers, bank robbers, and embezzlers. Since the early '60s, female arrests for major crimes have skyrocketed. The burgeoning number of women who are committing burglary, robbery, larceny and embezzlement is a disturbing side effect, I believe, of the steady erosion of the social and psychological differences between men and women. As the social status of women approaches that of men, so, I predict, will the frequency and nature of their crimes.

This dark side of the movement for full equality has been overlooked by everyone, including the scientific community. . . . But patterns are beginning to surface that are too clear to ignore. . . .

"Why Didn't I Take Cadillacs?"

Like her sisters in legitimate work, the female criminal is fighting for her niche in the hierarchy. She knows too

[3] From article by Freda Adler, associate professor, School of Criminal Justice, Rutgers—The State University. *Psychology Today.* 9:42–8. N. '75. Adapted from Chapter 1 of *Sisters in Crime: The Rise of the New Female Criminal* by Freda Adler. Copyright © 1975 by Freda Adler. Used with permission of McGraw-Hill Book Company.

much now to return to her former role as a second-rate criminal, confined to such "feminine" crimes as shoplifting and prostitution.

One inmate of a California institution puts it this way: "I needed more money, you know, and I was always taking these small transistor radios because there was this guy who would take all the radios I could give him for five or 10 dollars each. So I needed more money for drugs, and the only thing I could think of at first was 'take more radios.' Then one day it hit me. Wow! It was weird. What the hell was I doing just taking radios all these months? . . . I got with a friend—she was strung out too—and we started taking color TV sets . . . I can see it now . . . how dumb I was. I mean, if I was going to rip something off, why the hell didn't I take Cadillacs for all that time instead of some goddamned radios?"

Women's appetites are whetted when they successfully commit traditionally male crimes. "Crime is like anything else," explains a Los Angeles police lieutenant. "People learn and explore wider areas as they go along and gain confidence. You know how it is with a child . . . you can watch it grow and develop. It's like that with women we're getting. First it was a shock to be getting so many females. Now it's repeaters. You can see them grow in confidence. Like they opened a new door and realized all of a sudden that they can walk through it. The second time, they don't hesitate; they barge right in. . . . They'll go into the slammer with the others, and they learn to be better criminals. It's started now and you can't break the cycle. You can only wish it hadn't started."

An idea of the magnitude of the problem emerges from the FBI's yearly *Uniform Crime Reports,* the closest thing we have to a comprehensive national overview of crime. During the 12 years from 1960 through 1972, the FBI monitored 2,430 law-enforcement agencies across the country. They recorded the number and causes for all arrests. The startling finding was that the arrest rate among females was rising nearly three times faster than that of males.

In 12 years, the number of women arrested for robbery rose by 277 percent, while the male figure rose 169 percent. Embezzlement was up 280 percent for women, 50 percent for men; larceny up 303 percent for women, 82 percent for men. And there were 168 percent more women burglars in 1972 than in 1960; the percent of male burglars rose only 63 percent.

Weapons: Window Dressing

Except for comparable increases in murder and aggravated assault for men and women, the picture of female-arrest rates rising several times faster than male rates is a consistent one. Apparently the liberated female criminal, like her male counterpart, is more interested in improving her financial circumstances than in committing violence.

A 38-year-old parolee in Miami explains her interest in money rather than blood. "I had a gun when I went into this one place . . . it was a motel. But I never would have used it. I wanted the cash. I didn't want to hurt anyone. . . . It's a transaction between you and a large institution. There is no reason why [employees] should get hurt. I think most of the people in the joint [jail] work the same way. . . . Most of us are just in it for the bread. That's all. Guns, knives and the rest are a sort of necessary window dressing . . . which at times can get out of hand."

If adult-arrest rates say something about what is happening to American women now, the crime rates for girls under 18 say the future is even more worrisome. Between 1960 and 1972, the *Uniform Crime Reports* show a 508 percent jump in robbery arrests among girls under 18 while that for boys rose only half that much. There was a similar pattern for other offenses. Larceny was up 334 percent for girls, 84 percent for boys; burglary up 177 percent for girls, 70 percent for boys; auto theft 110 percent for girls, 38 percent for boys.

But similar to their adult counterparts, there was no significant difference between boys and girls in the increase of arrests for murder. Again, this suggests that economic rather than violent goals govern crime, an apparent bright spot in an otherwise bleak picture.

It has now become quite common for adolescent girls to participate in muggings, burglaries, and extortion rings that prey on schoolmates. The most telling sign of change at this level is gang membership. Gang activity is no longer all-male; girls now participate in all gang activities. In New York City, in fact, there are currently two all-girl gangs. . . .

Demanding Addicts

In the U.S., the trend suggests that the present rise in juvenile-female crime will increase rather than slacken. During one year (1971–1972) the FBI reported that arrest rates for serious crimes among girls under 18 climbed six percent in urban areas while the rates for boys actually dropped by one percent. In the suburbs, the picture was more ominous; female arrests for major crimes increased by 14 percent while the male rate eased back by two-tenths of a percent. It looks as if what the police, FBI, and even taxi drivers report now is likely to become aggravated in the future.

One cabbie in New York, headed out of Bedford-Stuyvesant, tells it his way: "I know the law says you gotta take fares anywhere, but not me. I don't get killed to collect a salary for nobody. And it ain't just men. Twice I've had women trying to pull something on me in the last year. They had guns, the whole works. And that ain't just me talking. Go see the other drivers . . . see if they ain't been hit by women. . . . Men, women, they're all the same. Don't trust none of them."

In New York at the police administration building on Broome Street, Lieutenant Lucy Acerra, a 20-year veteran of the force and now coordinator of the eight precincts in the city that have female officers, tells a similar story: "Now today, the majority of the women you see are narcotic addicts. But even they have changed . . . their attitude about themselves, the world. Years ago, you'd have a female addict, she'd be docile, almost embarrassed. Very quiet. Today . . . they come in the door screaming and never let up. They are much more demanding than ever before."

Not far away from Acerra's office, a New York assistant district attorney shakes his head while talking about how the city recently apprehended its first female loan shark: "That was something new. That was strictly an organized crime thing in the past. She was a freelancer, though. Even today, you don't get women operating on that level with the mob. They wouldn't stand for it. In a lot of ways they are a very conservative bunch of guys."

Soft Skin, Hard Muscle

Indeed, the Mafia has a long way to go before it can be considered an equal-opportunity employer or before we are likely to see a family "godmother." But the status of Mafia women may change. The mob, like any successful organization, reacts to competition and accomplishment. They are not likely to ignore the increasing number of women who are using guns, knives and wits to establish themselves as full partners, just as capable of violence and aggression as any man.

Popular culture has caught up fast with women's new willingness to reach for an equalizer. Movie stars, notably blacks, are turning martial arts, hat pins, groin kicks, and gun butts into cash at the box office. Films such as *Foxy Brown, Coffy,* and *Savage Sisters* slam home the point that under soft skin lies hard muscle.

Eight years ago the women of America passed something of a milestone in their criminal development. The first made her way onto the FBI's "10-most-wanted" list. But the novelty soon wore off. Five months after Ruth Eisemann-Schier appeared on the list for her part in a kidnap-killing, Marie Dean Arringon, an escaped murderer, made it to the top 10. Since then, it has become commonplace for a woman's name to be on the list for bank robbery, murder, kidnaping, or a variety of violent, revolutionary acts.

Another major turning point for American women may

have been the bizarre, tumultuous and, it turns out, short-lived era of the Symbionese Liberation Army (SLA). It symbolized the movement of radical females away from their quiescent participation in radical politics. By the 1970s, an increasing number of radical women were stirring a revolution within a revolution. True, they were still after urban social change, but they also wanted equality within the movement. In the early '70s the media noted with a good deal of humor the change in name of the violence-prone "Weathermen" to the unisex "Weather Underground." It was no longer humorous, however, when that same revolutionary feminism began to show up in the persons of such women as Nancy Ling Perry, Patricia Soltysik and Camilla Hall. These three women, all white, middle class, and highly educated, were at the core of the SLA. Along with their barrage of rhetoric and the kidnaping of Patricia Hearst, they ravaged banks, robbed commercial establishments, and helped plan assassinations with cyanide-tipped bullets.

"I Wanted a Bit of Easy Time"

. . . Women are no longer acting like subhuman primates with only one option. Medical, educational, economic, political and technological advances have freed them from unwanted pregnancies and provided them with male occupational skills. Weapons equalized their strength. It should be no surprise that, once armed with male opportunities, women should strive for status in criminal as well as legal pursuits. Women have always had the same aspirations as the dominant class, but lacking direct means, they have utilized ploys, ruses and indirection. Their resort to petty social gambits and petty crimes was a reflection more of their petty strengths than the pettiness of their ambitions.

We should not assume, however, that women who are committing what used to be "masculine" crimes are necessarily either members or supporters of the women's movement. Often they are the last persons in the world to credit their actions to any sort of liberation. Marge is typical of the new female criminal in both her actions and social values.

Before she was arrested for robbery, Marge had spent a good many years earning a living as a waitress or barmaid and raising two sons. When her husband deserted her, she decided to supplement her income. She thought first about becoming a prostitute, but felt she was too plump to be successful. She turned to shoplifting, and "boosting" from department stores became a regular habit. Then five years ago she hit upon the idea of robbing a bank. As she tells it, "I wanted a bit of easy time . . . the kids were getting older and I was still working and, after all those years, I needed a break. I guess maybe I got the idea from watching TV or something. I don't remember. But it surprised me; like, I first thought of it seriously and thought, 'No, I couldn't do that . . . I'm a woman,' you know? But when I thought more about it, what the hell, it didn't seem so bad. . . ." Marge robbed three banks before she was apprehended. She is now serving an indefinite sentence.

Marge comes from a low socioeconomic class and has traditional values about the place of women in society. She will not tolerate the mention of women's liberation because she thinks its members are lesbians. Her views are typical of most female offenders found in our nation's prisons. The traditional views of these women convince prison administrators, police officials and other law enforcement authorities that the women's movement is in no way connected to the sharply rising crime rate.

There is, however, an ever-growing national awareness of women's rights that is perhaps best described as the "new feminism." It is not an organized movement; it does not hold meetings or press conferences. It is an all-pervasive rise in female awareness that has permeated virtually every level of womanhood in America, at all ages. Today women believe they have more options, that they can do things that will change their lives, that they have the wherewithal to improve their economic status.

The new feminism pertains to women who may deny any sympathy for the formalized movement. It applies to those who have recently secured their first job, robbed their first bank, or snatched their first purse. It applies to women who staunchly defend their right to be feminine in the traditional sense. It affects women who have concluded that prostitution and shoplifting are beneath their dignity and their abilities.

The entrance of women into the major leagues of crime underscores the fact that the frequency and types of crime are more closely associated with social rather than sexual factors. As women rise socially, they become more visible in positions of prestige on both the legal and illegal sides of the fence. Old mental sets of devaluation and self-contempt gradually yield to new ones of pride, and sometimes an overcompensating arrogance.

The journey, so to speak, has just begun. The closer women approach the social and economic status of men, the more the two sexes will act alike. This is not to suggest that there are no inherent differences between the sexes. But these differences are not of prime importance in understanding female criminality. In the final analysis, women criminals are human beings who have basic needs and abilities and opportunities. Over the years their needs have not changed. The change has come in their abilities and opportunities—and aspirations. As options and hopes rise, I believe, we will see a kaleidoscope of social patterns whose final configuration will be different from any that modern society has ever known.

A CRIME THAT MADE
EVERYONE FEEL BETTER[4]

The old Brink's robbers were at this long table at Frankie and Johnny's on W. 45th St., demolishing lamb

[4] Article entitled "2 Losers at Brinksmanship Salute JFK Caper," by Pete Hamill, columnist. New York *Daily News*. p 3+. D. 13, '78. © 1978 by New York *Daily News*. Reprinted by permission.

chops and steaks, and talking about the Lufthansa job. It was a beautiful moment, with the two master craftsmen speaking the way Joe DiMaggio must sometimes talk about Pete Rose.

"Let's see how much it really is," said Jazz Maffie, a heavyset, 70-year-old, cigar-smoking semi-retired bookmaker. "They always start with these big numbers. The people that get robbed like to make it sound like a mint so they can get a bigger payoff from the insurance companies. By tomorra mornin', that $5 million might be a hundred and change."

Sandy Richardson, slight, white-haired, 72 years old, with eyes that sometimes turn to hardness, smiled thinly.

"They must've planned well," he said. "You can't pull off a major job without planning. That's why we could do what we did. We did the planning right."

The Lufthansa job seemed to make everybody in the city feel better yesterday, with the possible exceptions of the company and the cops. For one thing, it worked. We live in an era when a President tape-recorded his own felonies; when heroic Special Forces troops invaded the wrong prison camp; when terrorists have set fire to the wrong house in Brighton Beach and 31 FBI men somehow lost a kidnaper in the Pan Am Building. The five men who pulled the Lufthansa job did not make mistakes, and that is one reason people felt a little better when they heard the news.

"If they pull it off, I say hats off," said Jazz Maffie. "That's why they always liked us. That is why they made a movie about us. We got away with it." He took a drag on a cigar. "Well, for a long time."

The men who robbed Brink's of $1.2 million in cash in 1950 did get away with it for a long time, until a stool pigeon named Specs O'Keefe turned them in, and most of them ended up in the can. Jazz Maffie and Sandy Richardson got out of jail six years ago. O'Keefe died of heart failure at 67, somewhere in California a few years ago. He was called "Paul Williams" on the death certificate.

"Guys like O'Keefe, you always have to look out for," said Richardson. "And that's one of the problems, in that line of work. The planning can be perfect. But you don't know what people are really like. The guys on this Lufthansa job, now they'll see."

Suddenly, It's Over

"A guy falls in love with the wrong broad," said Maffie, "and it's all over. Some other guy gets stewed and starts talkin' big, and it's all over. Some guy can't wait to start spendin' the money, and suddenly he's got a Mercedes where he used to have a Ford and, forget it, it's over."

The weak link in the Brink's job was Specs O'Keefe, who had been a suspect from the day of the robbery. At one point, four years after the robbery, a New York hoodlum named Elmer (Trigger) Burke was imported to kill O'Keefe, who had been talking too much about the job. Burke staked out O'Keefe for six weeks, and one dark night jumped out of a sedan with a machine gun. He fired 40 rounds at O'Keefe, wounded him in the chest and arm, but didn't kill him. The cops later caught Burke with the machine gun and, when he had recovered, O'Keefe started to sing in full voice, and indictments were made five days before the statute of limitations would have run out.

When it was all over (Burke was sprung from the Charles St. jail in spectacular fashion, but died in the electric chair at Sing Sing for another crime a few years later), O'Keefe drifted to California, and Richardson, Maffie and six others went to jail. The other night, Richardson did not sound like a man who approved of killing anybody, even a stool pigeon.

"What would be the point?" he said. "Guys like that, you're better letting them live with themselves. They know what they did. They know they will die as rats. Let them live with themselves, if they can."

Some Deep Streak

Richardson felt also that ordinary citizens end up liking bank robbers because of some deep streak in human nature.

"Everybody's got some larceny in them," he said. "Watch people when they make a call from a pay phone. They put in the dime, they make the call and, when it's over, what do they do? They put their finger in the change slot. You think if the dime comes out they will mail it to the phone company? Of course not. Everybody likes stealing. Look at all the great books. In prison I read books, I even wrote two novels, and I helped reorganize the library —I put it on the Dewey Decimal System. And what is in all the great books? A crime. Somewhere there is always a crime in a great book. That's why people still want to know about us. It's years later, and they are standing on line to see the movie. They look at us, and they must figure what the hell, they didn't do anything worse than Nixon did."

Richardson and Maffie seemed amused at their sudden emergence from the past, and Maffie, at least, was slightly embarrassed. Later in the evening, when we had moved uptown to another place, he had a Scotch and soda and talked about it.

"What is this, being a celebrity?" he said. "We were thieves. We knocked off a joint, and that's all. But now people want our autographs. The cops knocked our heads together, and people want our autographs."

Wasn't a Fruit Stand

"You did something big, that's why," someone said. "It wasn't like knocking off a fruit stand."

"Well, that's true. It was big all right."

Richardson said: "It's just human nature. People like thieves."

Now that it was over, and they had done their time, Maffie and Richardson could afford to remember the funnier things about the Brink's job.

"Yeah, we could kid around during a job," Richardson

said. "You know, there's a lot of tension in that line of work. And if you got too much tension, sometimes it screws up the work. So someone would crack a joke, make everyone laugh, and you could keep working."

"That (Anthony) Pino," said Maffie. "He was a joker."

Drove FBI Nuts

"He drove the FBI nuts," Richardson said. "They had him staked out for months. And he'd be in his house, late at night, and then he'd come out and get in the car and drive. He'd go down along the highway, across the bridge, right into Scollay Square, where he jumps out of the car, and runs across the street—and buys a newspaper! Then he gets back in the car and drives home. With the feds after him all the way. Other times, 3 in the morning, he would sneak out to the car, ease it backwards out of the driveway with the lights out, slide into the street, and then put all the lights on and drive like a lunatic all around the neighborhood, with the feds going crazy trying to keep up, and then he'd just head home, park the car and go to bed. He was something."

Did they think the FBI was already shadowing suspects in the Lufthansa job?

"Undoubtedly," said Richardson. "There are only a few people in the whole country who are any good at this kind of thing."

Uh, where were Richardson and Maffie at 3:15 Monday morning, when the black Ford Econoline van pulled into Building 261 at Kennedy airport?

"In bed," Maffie said. "Exhausted from our labors." He took a drag from the cigar. "A German airline," he said. "Well, I hope it was Jewish thieves."

Richardson just smiled.

II. WHO DEFINES CRIME?
WHO MEASURES IT?

EDITOR'S INTRODUCTION

Crime is unsettling. It upsets the stability of neighborhoods, puts citizens on edge, limits the mobility of older persons who fear to leave their homes not just at night, but in broad daylight as well.

The problem isn't made any easier by the fact that experts disagree on the relative gravity of certain crimes, and that no one is really sure how large the problem of crime really is. Is the illegal dumping of waste chemicals that are known to cause cancer more criminal, or less criminal, than the murder of one drug dealer by another? How long is the "dark shadow" of unreported crime—and how does *not* knowing the answer affect the ways we think about crime and react to it as individuals and as a society?

These questions provide a useful backdrop to this section on crime and its measurement. In an article that originally appeared in *Daedalus*, Marvin E. Wolfgang, one of the most noted criminologists in the United States, points out that though crime may be what its beholder says it is, most people would agree that certain offenses are more grave than others. The U.S. crime rate is based on the reported incidence of the seven types of crime which the FBI deems most serious. The second excerpt, from the annual FBI report on crime, lists those crimes and 22 others, along with their official definitions. The third article, a press release issued by the FBI on the publication of its figures for 1977, surveys the fluctuating levels of "index crimes" since 1973.

In the next selection, Richard Lyons, a reporter for

the New York *Times,* comments on the completeness and accuracy of the FBI's figures. Lyons believes that crime statistics provide a distorted picture of crime and are all too easily misinterpreted.

William K. Stevens, in another New York *Times* article, tries to make sense of the latest crime figures. Crime seems to be rising in newly affluent areas, he feels, possibly for the simple reason that in those areas there are suddenly more goods to steal. And in the final piece, from the book *Criminal Violence, Criminal Justice,* Charles E. Silberman looks on two centuries of crime in America and reminds us that "the level of crime has always been high in the United States."

DEVIANCE AND CRIME[1]

The definition of crime is culturally subjective. So is society's response to persons who commit crimes. Crime is an act that is believed to be socially harmful by a group that has power to enforce its beliefs and that provides negative sanctions to be applied to persons who commit these acts. Although crime, like pornography, may be in the eye of the beholder, subjective perceptions about crime are closer to universality and retain a more temporal stability than do definitions of obscenity and pornography.

At least this generalization apples to serious crime and the meaning of seriousness. Acts that are defined in American culture as crimes which contain no personal victims and which do not involve physical injury, theft, or damage to property have a wider range of perceived seriousness; acts that involve injury, theft, or damage have a narrower

[1] From article entitled "Real and Perceived Changes of Crime and Punishment," by Marvin E. Wolfgang, author, professor of sociology and law, and director, Center for Studies in Criminology and Criminal Law, University of Pennsylvania. *Daedalus.* 107:143–157. Copyright © 1978 by the American Academy of Arts and Sciences. Reprinted by permission of DAEDALUS, Journal of the American Academy of Arts and Sciences, Boston, Massachusetts. Winter 1978, A New America?

range of seriousness and considerable stability over time in their rank order of gravity.

It is commonplace to refer to the cultural relativity of crime and to mention that the crime of yesteryear is noncriminal today. What is less trite and certainly not trivial is Emile Durkheim's notion that crime is normal, not pathological. Durkheim said that even in a society of saints there would still be crime, by which he meant that if all acts we know as crime were eliminated, small differences in behavior that now appear to have no moral significance would take on a new and important meaning. Slight breaches of manners and good taste could become serious crimes.

In his terms, crime involves acts that offend strong collective moral sentiments. If these sentiments weaken, then what were formerly considered to be serious offenses would be considered less serious; when the sentiments grow stronger, less serious offenses are promoted to a more serious category. The degrees of enforcement and severity of sanctions are correlated with the intensity and degree of commitment to the collective moral sentiments.

Even though deviance may have both inevitability and elasticity, we are currently experiencing in America, perhaps in Western society, an expansion of acceptability of deviance and a corresponding contraction of what we define as crime. The total quantity of criminal and noncriminal deviance may be constant, both in value definitions and in statistical frequency; but the line of demarcation between criminal and noncriminal deviance is being positioned at a different point in the total line segment we call deviance.

By a contraction of what is deemed delinquent, the criminal law will be made more enforceable. The more narrow range of behavior considered criminal will mean a stronger link of consistency with history, for the persistently serious offenses like homicide, rape, and thefts, which have almost everywhere and always been viewed as criminal,

will constitute the hard core of criminality, and the actors
will continue to be viewed as criminals.

The Increase and Decrease of Crimes of Violence

Since 1930, the major method for determining the
amount of crime in the United States has been the Uniform
Crime Reports (UCR) of the Federal Bureau of Investigation. These annual reports are produced from the collection
of police reports in departments of cities and county
jurisdictions across the country. There are twenty-nine
categories of offenses, but only the first seven are used for
what is known as a crime index, a classification analogous to
the consumer price index, the cost of living index, and the
index of economic productivity. These seven include criminal homicide, forcible rape, robbery, aggravated assault,
burglary, larceny of $50 and over, and automobile theft,
and are referred to as "offenses known to the police." All
the remaining twenty-two offense categories are reported
only in terms of the number of persons arrested.

There has been much critical commentary over the
past forty-five years about the validity of the crime index,
both from traditional scholars who use the crime index reports and from Marxists who deride the data and deny the
validity of a capitalist system that fails to take into account
the criminogenic forces of the economic and political power
of the state. Putting aside those issues and admitting that
except for the new series of data known as "victimization
rates," collected by the Bureau of the Census in cooperation with the Law Enforcement Assistance Administration,
there is little other basis . . . scholars or public officials
have for determining whether crime rates are increasing,
decreasing, or remaining stable.

Using the [1977] UCR data, it can be said that since
1960 crimes of violence have increased 180 percent. The
fear of crime, as indicated in a variety of localized studies,
has probably increased in even greater proportions than
the recorded reality of crime. That many crimes are un-
recorded, that reporting procedures have varied over this

time, and that more crimes may be reported now—particularly rape—than in earlier days are issues that are difficult to test empirically.

Nonetheless, there appears to be some consensus among the community of criminologists who examine criminal statistics that the amount of real criminality has considerably and significantly increased during the past fifteen years. That there have been equally high rates of crime and crimes of violence recorded in earlier eras of the history of the United States has been asserted by using such long-time series data as Buffalo and Boston provide and as are recorded in the Task Force Reports of the National Commission on the Causes and Prevention of Violence. Crimes of violence in the latter part of the nineteenth century were as high or higher than even the currently reported rates of crimes of violence.

The issue, however, is that within the memories of the current living population of the United States, since the early 1960s, there has been such an upsurge in crimes of violence, or street crimes, that social concern, governmental budgets, and public policy are increasingly affected.

OFFENSES IN UNIFORM CRIME REPORTING[2]

Offenses in Uniform Crime Reporting are divided into two groupings designated as Part I and Part II offenses. Crime Index offenses are included among the Part I offenses. Offense and arrest information are reported for the Part I offenses on a monthly basis, whereas only arrest information is reported for Part II offenses.

The Part I offenses are as follows:

1. Criminal homicide.— (a) Murder and non-negligent manslaughter: all willful felonious homicides as distinguished from deaths caused by negligence, and excludes

[2] From *Uniform Crime Reports for the United States, 1977.* United States Department of Justice. Federal Bureau of Investigation. Washington, DC 20535, '78. p 304–5.

attempts to kill, assaults to kill, suicides, accidental deaths, or justifiable homicides. Justifiable homicides are limited to: (1) the killing of a felon by a law enforcement officer in line of duty; and (2) the killing of a person in the act of committing a felony by a private citizen. (b) Manslaughter by negligence [not included in the Crime Index]: any death which the police investigation established was primarily attributable to gross negligence of some individual other than the victim.

2. Forcible rape.—The carnal knowledge of a female forcibly and against her will in the categories of rape by force and attempts or assaults to rape. Excludes statutory offenses (no force used—victim under age of consent).

3. Robbery.—Stealing or taking anything of value from the care, custody, or control of a person by force or by violence or by putting in fear, such as strong-arm robbery, stickups, armed robbery, attempts or assaults to rob.

4. Aggravated assault.—Assault with intent to kill or for the purpose of inflicting severe bodily injury by shooting, cutting, stabbing, maiming, poisoning, scalding, or by the use of acids, explosives, or other means. Excludes simple assaults.

5. Burglary—breaking or entering.—Housebreaking or any breaking or unlawful entry of a structure with the intent to commit a felony or a theft. Includes attempted forcible entry.

6. Larceny-theft (except motor vehicle theft).—The unlawful taking, carrying, leading, or riding away of property from the possession or constructive possession of another. Thefts of bicycles, automobile accessories, shoplifting, pocket-picking, or any stealing of property or article which is not taken by force and violence or by fraud. Excludes embezzlement, "con" games, forgery, worthless checks, etc.

7. Motor vehicle theft.—Unlawful taking or attempted theft of a motor vehicle. A motor vehicle is self-propelled and travels on the surface rather than on rails. Specifically excluded from this category are motorboats, construction equipment, airplanes, and farming equipment.

The Part II offenses are:

8. Other assaults (simple).—Assaults which are not of an aggravated nature and where no weapon is used.

9. Arson.—Willful or malicious burning with or without intent to defraud. Includes attempts.

10. Forgery and counterfeiting.—Making, altering, uttering or possessing, with intent to defraud, anything false which is made to appear true. Includes attempts.

11. Fraud.—Fraudulent conversion and obtaining money or property by false pretenses. Includes bad checks except forgeries and counterfeiting. Also includes larceny by bailee.

12. Embezzlement.—Misappropriation or misapplication of money or property entrusted to one's care, custody, or control.

13. Stolen property; buying, receiving, possessing.—Buying, receiving, and possessing stolen property, including attempts.

14. Vandalism.—Willful or malicious destruction, injury, disfigurement, or defacement of property without consent of the owner or person having custody or control.

15. Weapons; carrying, possessing, etc.—All violations of regulations or statutes controlling the carrying, using, possessing, furnishing, and manufacturing of deadly weapons or silencers. Includes attempts.

16. Prostitution and commercialized vice.—Sex offenses of a commercialized nature and attempts, such as prostitution, keeping a bawdy house, procuring, or transporting women for immoral purposes.

17. Sex offenses (except forcible rape, prostitution, and commercialized vice).—Statutory rape, offenses against chastity, common decency, morals, and the like. Includes attempts.

18. Drug abuse violations.—Offenses relating to narcotic drugs, such as unlawful possession, sale, use, growing, and manufacturing of narcotic drugs.

19. Gambling.—Promoting, permitting, or engaging in illegal gambling.

20. Offenses against the family and children.—Nonsupport, desertion, or abuse of family and children.

21. Driving under the influence.—Driving or operating any motor vehicle or common carrier while drunk or under the influence of liquor or narcotics.

22. Liquor laws.—State or local liquor law violations, except "drunkenness" (class 23) and "driving under the influence" (class 21). Excludes Federal violations.

23. Drunkenness.—Drunkenness or intoxication.

24. Disorderly conduct.—Breach of the peace.

25. Vagrancy.—Vagabondage, begging, loitering, etc.

26. All other offenses.—All violations of state or local laws, except classes 1–25 and traffic.

27. Suspicion.—No specific offense; suspect released without formal charges being placed.

28. Curfew and loitering laws.—Offenses relating to violation of local curfew or loitering ordinances where such laws exist.

29. Runaway.—Limited to juveniles taken into protective custody under provisions of local statutes.

HOW MUCH CRIME IN THE U.S.?[3]

Crime reported to law enforcement agencies across the country declined 3 percent in 1977, Attorney General Griffin B. Bell announced today [October 18, 1978].

The Crime Index of the Federal Bureau of Investigation's *Uniform Crime Reports*—used to measure the fluctuation in crime nationwide—indicated the decrease from 1976, when an estimated 11,304,800 offenses occurred. In 1977, the total was down to 10,935,800 Index crimes reported. In the same period, the U.S. population increased 1 percent.

Collectively, the Index's property crimes of burglary, larceny-theft, and motor vehicle theft fell 4 percent in

[3] Press release, issued by the Federal Bureau of Investigation. United States Department of Justice. Washington, DC 20535. O. 18, '78.

volume. Conversely, the total number of violent crimes of murder, forcible rape, robbery, and aggravated assault increased 2 percent. Among the Index offenses that declined, larceny-theft dropped 6 percent, robbery was down 4 percent, and burglary fell 1 percent. Those showing increases were: forcible rape, 11 percent; aggravated assault, 6 percent; murder, 2 percent; and motor vehicle theft, 1 percent.

These final 1977 figures are contained in the FBI's annual publication, "Crime in the United States," released today by FBI Director William H. Webster. Mr. Webster said the publication is the result of a cooperative effort of nearly 15,000 law enforcement agencies and represents the most comprehensive study of our Nation's crime available today.

When comparing the 1977 experience with that of 1973, the volume of Index crimes in the Nation increased 25 percent. As a group, the violent crimes rose 15 percent, and the property crimes were up 27 percent.

In 1977, reported crime in cities with populations over 250,000 declined 6 percent from the 1976 total. Decreases were also recorded in both the suburban and rural areas, 3 and 1 percent, respectively.

The 1977 crime rate of 5,055 Index offenses per 100,000 U.S. inhabitants relates the volume of reported crime to population. This rate showed a decline of 4 percent from the 1976 experience, but a 22-percent increase over the 1973 rate. In 1977, the violent crime rate per 100,000 inhabitants was up 2 percent over the 1976 rate and 12 percent over the 1973 figure. The property crime rate per 100,000 inhabitants fell 5 percent during 1977 from 1976, but when compared with the 1973 figure, a 23-percent increase was shown.

Geographically, all regions recorded decreases in total Crime Index offenses reported during 1977 as compared to 1976. The North Central States reported a 6-percent decline; the Northeastern States, 4 percent; the Southern States, 2 percent; and the Western States, 1 percent.

Law enforcement agencies were successful in clearing

21 percent of the Index crimes reported during 1977. Twenty-eight percent of these clearances involved only the arrests of persons under 18 years of age. Regionally, the highest overall Crime Index clearance rate was recorded by the Southern States with 24 percent.

An estimated 10.2 million arrests for all criminal acts except traffic violations were made by law enforcement agencies in 1977. Actual arrests were down less than 1 percent from 1976 and up 4 percent over 1973. The 1977 arrest rate per 1,000 inhabitants was 47 for the Nation as a whole, 67 in cities with more than 250,000 inhabitants, 39 in the suburban areas, and 32 in the rural areas.

In 1977, persons under the age of 18 accounted for 24 percent of the arrestees, those under 21 for 40 percent, and those under 25 for 56 percent. Male arrests for all ages outnumbered those of females by 5 to 1.

Eighty percent of the adults arrested for Crime Index offenses during the year were prosecuted in the courts. Of these, 68 percent were found guilty as charged, 8 percent were convicted of a lesser offense, and the remaining 24 percent were released either through acquittal or dismissal. Of all persons processed for Index crimes, 41 percent were young persons referred to a juvenile court jurisdiction.

As of October 31, 1977, 10,879 agencies, representing a population of more than 201 million, reported employing 437,000 full-time law enforcement officers or an average of 2.2 per 1,000 inhabitants. When full-time civilians were included, the total was 545,000 employees for an average of 2.7 for each 1,000.

FUZZY CRIME STATISTICS[4]

The national crime rate takes as many twists and turns as the Dow-Jones Industrial Average. It may be up, down or

[4] Article by Richard Lyons, reporter. New York *Times*. Sec. IV, p 6. S. 18, '77. © 1977 by The New York Times Company. Reprinted by permission.

sideways, depending on the perceptions and prejudices of both the compilers and the beholders, and almost any interpretation can be justified because the collection of crime statistics throughout the country is acknowledged to be a mess by almost everyone in law enforcement and the administration of justice. Former Attorney General Edward H. Levi stated last year [1976] that national crime data was of questionable validity, and his successor, Griffin B. Bell, now is attempting to do something about it.

On Mr. Bell's order, the Justice Department is hatching a plan that would, if implemented, seek not only to find out in precise detail what crimes are committed, where, when and by whom, but also to interpret the information in ways that would help detect trends and use them in preventing crime. The proposal for an agency to collect and analyze data about crime is hardly new. As long ago as 1870 a provision calling for such an office was contained in the act that established the Justice Department, and in the ensuing century a dozen Federal and private commissions and committees have recommended a Federal crime data agency similar to the national Center for Health Statistics, created in 1960.

The main concerns of the attorneys who run the Justice Department, which itself has been described as "one big law firm," have been to draft legislation, interpret laws and prosecute violators, not to gather statistical data and certainly not to try to analyze it. The inexact science of criminology itself is relatively new and its theoretical segment has yet to penetrate the Federal bureaucracy.

But the biggest deterrent to the creation of a crime statistics agency has been the inaccuracy of the data itself. The F.B.I.'s annual report, "Crime in the United States," is merely a compilation of serious crimes submitted to the bureau by the nation's 11,000 local police agencies. Most attention is paid to seven categories: murder, forcible rape, robbery, aggravated assault, burglary, larceny-theft, and auto theft. The numbers themselves represent only those occasions when a citizen has chosen to tell the police that he has been victimized and when the local police department in turn has chosen to relay this information to the bureau.

The F.B.I.'s annual report is considerably distorted by the gross underreporting of crime to the police. Recent surveys conducted by the Census Bureau for the Justice Department estimate that for each serious criminal act that is reported, two or three others are not, in part because the victim believes it is futile to file complaints.

Another omission of the bureau's reports is their lack of attention to so-called white-collar crime. They do not include such criminal acts as a politician taking a bribe, a merchant cheating a customer, a lawyer swindling a client, or a physician injuring a patient while drunk. In any case, the police never learn about many white-collar crimes. It has been estimated, for example, that 90 percent of crimes involving computer manipulation are never reported.

Even murders sometimes go unreported because they are known only to the perpetrator. In three now widely-publicized cases in recent years murderers in Houston, Los Angeles and Vacaville, Calif., are believed to have killed a total of about 100 persons although the local police forces had been unaware of many of the slayings for years.

Even the definition of crimes can help fudge the numbers. Purse-snatching can be classed as either a robbery or a larceny, and a punch in the nose can be counted as an aggravated or a simple assault depending on motive.

Complicating the criminal numbers game is the variety of agencies playing it, even in the Justice Department. One departmental report notes that in the current fiscal year the department "will spend $64.1 million supporting 54 systems and programs located in 17 different divisions, bureaus, boards, etc., which produce, or are readily capable of producing, general purpose statistical series or which support the development of such programs at the state level."

The author of this report, Dr. Harry A. Scarr, a sociologist and administrator of the Federal Justice Research program, is critical of the present criminal data system and wants to change and amplify it. He says there is a need to improve the present system to the point at which a statistically valid "crime indicator" can be produced in much the same fashion as the statistics on the gross national product, consumer prices and unemployment.

"You can more intelligently combat crime if you know more accurately the size of the problem at hand by obtaining the best information possible and depoliticizing it," he says. "If crime of a certain kind is increasing in a certain region, certain policies can be adopted to fight it."

One method that could produce better numbers would expand the five-year-old National Crime Panel Survey, which interviews a sampling of citizens through polling techniques to find out if they have been victimized, under what conditions and whether the crimes have been reported to the police. This is an outgrowth of the Census Bureau's original survey, taken in 1970, which detected an enormous reservoir of unreported crime.

Dr. Scarr stressed that an equally important objective of a national crime data agency would be compiling statistics on the results of crime, especially on how charges are disposed of by the criminal justice system. At present there is no cohesive data about the numbers of crimes resulting in prosecutions, much less on convictions, sentences, time served in prison and recidivism.

"The data is going along different tracks. We need to unify the collection system, make it more accurate and include statistics from our courts and prisons," he says. "Right now almost all the time spent on crime data is devoted to gathering it, no one digests it and we do not know what a lot of it means."

CRIME RISING IN SOUTH AND WEST[5]

Violent crime and major theft, following a shift of people and money from the North and East, now appear to

[5] Article by William K. Stevens, reporter. New York *Times*. p 1+. D. 24, '78. © 1978 by The New York Times Company. Reprinted by permission.

be creating an increasingly grim counterpoint to the vigorous growth and gilt-edged prosperity of the South and
West.

A detailed analysis of the latest national crime reports
by the Federal Bureau of Investigation, some recently published and some unpublished, seems to confirm what some
criminologists have suspected: that the rate of serious crime
has eased off in much of the East and Middle West but has
risen in much of the Sun Belt and the West.

But the evidence must be interpreted cautiously, the
experts say. Some analysts suggest that the trend must be
watched longer before it can be determined that there has
been a long-term shift in criminal activity. And the pattern
is not uniform. Nonetheless, the statistics do seem to reveal
broad currents of change.

The incidence of major crimes—murder, [forcible] rape,
robbery, aggravated assault, burglary, larceny-theft and
automobile theft—increased by 4.9 percent in the United
States from 1974 to 1978. But in the industrial crescent of
the upper Middle West, historically a high-crime region, it
dropped by 1.9 percent.

In contrast, major crimes soared by 12.9 percent in the
region encompassing Texas, Oklahoma, Louisiana and Arkansas. In fact, the analysis suggests, but does not prove,
that greater Houston and Dallas-Fort Worth may have experienced the biggest jumps of any of the country's 25
largest metropolitan areas.

The major exception to the pattern was in the region
that includes New York, New Jersey and Pennsylvania,
where the incidence of serious crime increased by 16 percent.
This jump may be an artificial one, however, according to
the F.B.I. New York, which dominates the region nu-
merically, joined other states in 1975 in requiring local
police to report crimes. Reported crime may have increased as a result, it is felt, making the mid-Atlantic jump
more apparent than real.

The North-to-South and East-to-West shift tends to appear in an analysis of murder rates, too. Killing has de-

clined nationally, by 9.28 percent, since 1974, when the
most murders were reported. But it fell most sharply in the
industrial crescent, by 17.4 percent, and along the East
Coast south of Pennsylvania, by 24.4 percent. This contrasts
with a rise in the Pacific coastal region, where the incidence
of murder increased by 15.1 percent.

"Houston is the murder capital right now," says Dr.
Marvin E. Wolfgang, a University of Pennsylvania criminologist. And indeed, the analysis of F.B.I. figures indicates
that in the Houston metropolitan area, there were 18
killings for every 100,000 people in 1977. That ranked first
among the 25 largest metropolitan areas. New York, at 17.1,
ranked second. Dallas and Los Angeles joined Miami in the
top five, replacing Atlanta and Detroit. The latter two metropolitan areas ranked first and second in 1974.

More Major Crimes Reported

For the immediate future, raw figures on reported
crimes for the first nine months of 1978 . . . do not dis-
pute the trend, although they are unadjusted for population differences. The overall number of major crimes was
reported up in the central cities of Houston, San Diego,
Miami, San Francisco, Denver and Los Angeles, and down
in Detroit, New York, St. Louis, Chicago, Boston, Min-
neapolis and Newark. Houston's rate of increase, 12 percent, was the highest among major cities. Murders increased here by 26 percent.

Law-enforcement officials and criminologists have generally been unable to demonstrate provable reasons for
recent changes in the pattern and incidence of reported
crime. There are theories, however, and one of the most
frequently cited has been put forth by Dr. Wolfgang.

It says simply that serious crime is a function of youth,
that older people are less likely to commit criminal acts.
Therefore, the younger the population, the greater the likelihood of serious crime. Dr. Wolfgang attributes the drop
in crime in the North and East largely to a decrease in the
youth population.

Conversely, he said, younger people are being drawn to the prosperous Southern and Western cities by economic opportunity, and more of them are likely to be male than female. "Those demographics alone suggest that there would be an increase in crimes of violence," he said.

Money Draws Criminals

Further, he pointed out, money obviously draws criminals, and places like Houston and Dallas have plenty of money. "It's reminiscent of Willie Sutton's statement about why he robs banks: 'because that's where the money is,' " he said. In fact, robberies of banks and savings-and-loan institutions in Houston, while still much lower than in many other cities, have doubled this year.

Dr. Wolfgang said that the gun-oriented history of the Southwest is probably a factor, too. "Combine that with rapid urbanization and the demographics, and even if you didn't know Houston had a high homicide rate, you'd expect that it would."

Murder is considered one of the most reliable single guides to the true rate of violent crime because killings are nearly always discovered while instances of other crimes sometimes go unreported. . . .

Among a selected group of 20 large cities, every one in the Sun Belt and the West showed an increase in serious crime from 1974 to 1978, except for Miami. Among these were San Francisco, San Diego, Denver, Houston, Dallas, Atlanta and Los Angeles.

Some Northern and Eastern cities recorded jumps, too, among them New York, Cleveland, Milwaukee and Baltimore. But others, such as Detroit, Washington, St. Louis, Pittsburgh, Chicago and Philadelphia, recorded decreases.

Except for murder, Houston generally has had lower crime rates than many other large cities, but other forms of crime appear to be increasing. In 1977 for example, there were only 24 robberies of banks or savings-and-loan associations. As of Dec. 14, 51 had been reported in 1978.

After the incidence took a dramatic jump last summer, the Clearing House, Houston's banking association, began offering rewards for information leading to arrests. So far, according to a spokesman for the group, four robbers have been arrested as a result.

The Houston Police Department, which is considered substantially undermanned in the face of the city's explosive growth, is encouraging private citizens and organizations to take an active part in helping to stem the rise of crime. "We would thoroughly encourage them, whether they're a businessman or an individual, to take whatever preventive measures are available," said Rick Hartley, a department spokesman, noting that there is only so much that the police can do without citizen cooperation.

"The police department is just the report-card issuer," he said.

AS AMERICAN AS JESSE JAMES[6]

O I see flashing that this America is only you and me,
Its power, weapons, testimony are you and me,
Its crimes, lies, thefts, defections, are you and me . . .

> —WALT WHITMAN, 1865

Be not afraid of any man,
No matter what his size;
When danger threatens, call on me
And I will equalize.

> —INSCRIPTION ON THE NINETEENTH-
> CENTURY WINCHESTER RIFLE

"I seen my opportunities and I took 'em."

> —GEORGE WASHINGTON PLUNKETT
> OF TAMMANY HALL, C. 1900

[6] From *Criminal Violence, Criminal Justice*, by Charles E. Silberman, copyright © 1978 by Charles E. Silberman. p 21–36. Reprinted by permission of Random House, Inc. Charles E. Silberman is director of the Study of Law and Justice, a Ford Foundation research project.

I

"Men murdered themselves into this democracy," D. H. Lawrence wrote more than a half-century ago, in an essay on James Fenimore Cooper's *Leather-Stocking Tales*. An exaggeration, perhaps; but crime, violence, and lawlessness have been recurrent themes throughout American history. The continent was conquered by the musket, as well as by the ax and the plow. In the speech that first brought him to public attention, delivered in Springfield, Illinois, in January, 1838, Abraham Lincoln argued that internal violence was the nation's major domestic problem and decried "the increasing disregard for law that pervades the country." Little has changed since then; as the National Commission on the Causes and Prevention of Violence wrote in its 1969 report, "Violence has been far more intrinsic to our past than we should like to think."

The fact that violence has been one of the most durable aspects of the American experience offers no comfort to victims of crime, or to those who live in fear of being attacked. Nor is there consolation in knowing that the country was more dangerous in the past than it is now. But we cannot understand our current crime problem, let alone find remedies for it, without understanding the ways in which crime and violence are rooted in American life.

Since the colonies were first settled, each generation of Americans has felt itself threatened by the specter of rising crime and violence. In 1767, Benjamin Franklin, in his capacity as agent for Pennsylvania, petitioned the British Parliament to stop solving *its* crime problem by shipping convicted felons to the American colonies. Transported felons were corrupting the morals of the poor, Franklin complained, and terrorizing the rest of the population with the many burglaries, robberies, and murders they committed.

Crime continued to be a problem after the Republic was established, and Americans continued to attribute the problem to the current crop of immigrants, who were thought to be more given to crime than their predecessors. "Immigrants to the city are found at the bar of our criminal tribunals, in our bridewell, our penitentiary, and our state prison," the Managers of the Society for the Prevention of Pauperism in the City of New York reported in 1819. "And we lament to say that they are too often led by want, by vice, and by habit to form a phalanx of plunder and depredation, rendering our city more liable to the increase of crimes, and our houses of correction more crowded with convicts and felons."

Twenty years later, things seemed to have deteriorated further. "One of the evidences of the degeneracy of our morals and of the inefficiency of our police is to be seen in the frequent instances of murder by stabbing," Philip Hone, a former mayor of New York, wrote in his diary for December 2, 1839. Fear of crime was a tradition in every other city as well. In 1844, a Philadelphian wrote that people were arming themselves because experience taught them not to expect protection from the law. And just before the Civil War a U.S. Senate committee investigating crime in Washington, D.C., reported that "Riot and bloodshed are of daily occurrence, innocent and unoffending persons are shot, stabbed, and otherwise shamefully maltreated, and not infrequently the offender is not even arrested.

The law was even less effective in the South and West than it was in the East. In a single fifteen-month period in the 1850s, a total of forty-four murders were recorded in Los Angeles, then a town of only 8,000 inhabitants—about forty or fifty times as high as the city's current murder rate. The term "hoodlum" originated in San Francisco, to describe sadistic juveniles and young men who preyed on that city's Chinese population during the 1860s, robbing, raping, and torturing almost at will. In a typical exploit during the summer of 1868, a gang of hoodlums dragged a Chinese fisherman under a wharf, where they robbed him, beat him with a club, branded him in a dozen places with hot irons, then slit his ears and tongue.

During the first half of the nineteenth century, *all* cities were dangerous—those of Europe as well as the United States. In the second half, London, Paris, and other European cities were bringing crime and disorder under control, while American cities were not—or so it appeared to contemporary observers. New Yorkers are "even more dangerous" than Londoners, the American reformer Charles Loring Brace wrote in 1872, in *The Dangerous Classes of New York*. "They rifle a bank, where English thieves pick pockets; they murder, where European proletaires cudgel or fight with fists; in a riot they begin what seems about to be the sacking of a city, where English rioters would merely batter policemen or smash lamps." That same year, *Wood's Illustrated Handbook* warned visitors to New York not to walk around the city at night except in the busiest streets and urged them to take particular pains to avoid Central Park after sundown.

In the meantime, Chicago was already cementing its reputation as the nation's crime capital. In the 1860s, the Chicago *Tribune* gave the nickname "Thieves' Corner" to the intersection of Randolph and Dearborn streets. In the twenty years after the Civil War, the murder rate quadrupled, far outstripping the growth in population, and muggings were commonplace; in 1893, one Chicago resident in eleven was arrested for one crime or another.

Outside the cities, violence was very much on the increase. The family blood feud, virtually unknown before the Civil War, exploded into public view, kindled by hatreds generated during the war and refueled by political and economic conflicts. The Hatfield-McCoy feud was only one of a number of bloody Appalachian Mountain vendettas; equally deadly feuds were fought in Texas, Arizona, and New Mexico.

The second half of the nineteenth century was also the time when that indigenous American institution, the vigilante movement, flourished. Vigilantism was a response to the absence of law and order on the frontier. An Indiana vigilante group argued that "the people of this country are the real sovereigns, and whenever the laws, made by those to whom they have delegated their authority, are found inadequate to their protection, it is the right of the people to take the protection of their property into their own hands, and deal with these villains according to their just desserts [sic]. . . ." Vigilantism was initiated by frontiersmen who were inadequately protected by the law, but it gained support, and often leadership, from members of the American political, intellectual, and business elite. Governors, senators, judges, ministers, and even two presidents—Andrew Jackson and Theodore Roosevelt—were vigilantes or vigilante supporters.

Vigilantes found it hard to distinguish between taking the law into their hands when it could not function and taking the law into their hands when it did not function as they wanted it to. In the twentieth century, therefore, vigilante movements turned their attention away from horse thieves, cattle rustlers, counterfeiters, and assorted criminals and outlaws, and toward those whose only crime was to join a trade union or to belong to a different racial, ethnic, religious, or political group. Vigilante violence has had a strong conservative basis.

Vigilantism was one of the foundations on which the racial caste system was erected. Slavery began in violence, with the uprooting of Africans from their homes and their transportation first to the African coast, then to the New World; current estimates are that one-third of the Africans died en route to the ports of embarkation, and another third during the infamous "Middle Passage" to the United States. Slavery was maintained by violence; and when slavery ended, violence was used to keep blacks "in their place." In the late nineteenth century, after federal troops were withdrawn from the South, the white leadership made vigilante violence against blacks an integral part of the system of white supremacy they were erecting. Between 1882 and 1903, no fewer than 1,985 blacks were killed by Southern lynch mobs. And violence against blacks was not limited to mob action; individual acts of violence and terror became an accepted part of the caste system.

During this same period, a new kind of criminal emerged in the small towns and rural areas of the Midwest and South: the outlaw turned social hero. These "social bandits" included such people as Wild Bill Hickok; Billy the Kid, who sprang to fame during the Lincoln County war, one of the more spectacular of the New Mexico family feuds; and Jesse and Frank James, former Confederate guerrillas turned bank robbers and killers. The James brothers' criminal career is particularly instructive. During its fifteen-year existence, their gang held up at least eleven banks, seven railroad trains, three stagecoaches, and one county fair, for a total take estimated at a little under $250,000; during the course of these robberies, sixteen people were killed. This record of banditry made Jesse and Frank James popular heroes among Midwesterners who had been sympathetic to the Confederate cause, and they were lionized by the Midwestern press. When the James gang held up the Kansas City Fair in 1872, a Kansas City newspaper hailed the robbery as "so diabolically daring and so utterly in contempt of fear that we are bound to admire it and revere its perpetrators." Two days later, the paper compared the James brothers to the Knights of King Arthur's Round Table:

It was as though three bandits had come to us from storied Odenwald, with the halo of medieval chivalry upon their garments, and shown us how the things were done that poets sing of. Nowhere else in the United States or in the civilized world, probably, could this thing have been done.

To be sure, vicarious identification with outlaws seems to be a characteristic of modern societies. Robin Hood is a figure of English folklore, and American Western TV programs are popular the world over. Even so, the "evangelism of violence," as one critic calls it, has always held a peculiar fascination for Americans. "It seems quite possible that the place of Jesse James, Billy the Kid, and Wild Bill Hickok is as secure in the pantheon of American folk heroes as that of Bat Masterson and Wyatt Earp," the criminologists Gresham Sykes and Thomas Drabek have written. "We seem to remember our sheriffs and our outlaws with equal pleasure." One reason is that often it was hard to tell the difference between them; some of the most famous gunfighters worked both sides of the law, spending part of their careers as outlaws and part as lawmen, depending on which side offered the better opportunity. (We continue to romanticize the bandits of the post–Civil War era. Hollywood has made no fewer than twenty-one movies about Billy the Kid: in one version, the hero was played by Paul Newman, and in another, by Kris Kristofferson, although in real life Billy was described as "a slight, short, buck-toothed, narrow-shouldered youth" who "looks like a cretin." Gary Cooper played Wild Bill Hickok; and in the best of the various movies made about the James brothers, Jesse was played by Tyrone Power and Frank by Henry Fonda.)

Back in the cities, meanwhile, disrespect for law helped usher in the age of the "Robber Barons." Cornelius Vanderbilt expressed the outlook of other businessmen in replying to criticism of the way he had amassed his $90 million fortune. "What do I care about the law," he scoffed. "Hain't I got the power?" In a rapidly expanding, urbanizing, industrializing America, the only law to which the Robber Barons gave obeisance was "the law of the survival of the fittest."

The intelligence, imagination, and daring that characterized the Robber Barons carried over to a new breed of professional thieves who emerged at about the same time. Forgers, embezzlers, confidence men, burglars, and robbers captured the popular imagination in the East, much as the "social bandits" did in the South and West. "The ways of making a livelihood by crime are many, and the number of men and women who live by their wits in all large cities reaches into the thousands," Inspector Thomas Byrnes, Chief of Detectives of the New York City Police Department, wrote in 1886 in his often admiring volume *Professional Criminals of America.*

Some of the criminals are really very clever in their own peculiar line, and are constantly turning their thieving qualities to the utmost pecuniary account. Robbery is now classed as a profession, and in the place of the awkward and hang-dog looking thief we have today the thoughtful and intelligent rogue. There seems to be a strange fascination about crime that draws men of brains, and with their eyes wide open, into its meshes.

The most successful, hence most admired of this new breed of professional thief, were the safe-crackers, who specialized in robbing bank safes. "It requires rare qualities in a criminal to become an expert bank-safe robber," Byrnes observed. "The professional bank burglar must have patience, intelligence, mechanical knowledge, industry, determination, fertility of resources, and courage—all in high degree." The rewards were commensurate; the booming industrial economy, with its heavy demand for capital, meant that banks kept large sums of currency and negotiable government securities in their vaults. In terms of the scale of their operations and the amount of money taken, the big-city professional thieves made folk bandits such as the James brothers look like adolescent street muggers.

□ On April 6, 1869, "Big Frank" McCoy and his fellow safe-crackers stole $1 million in cash and government securities from the Catholic Beneficial Fund Bank of Philadelphia.

□ Two months later, Jimmy "Old Man" Hope, Ned Lyons, and others took $1.2 million from New York City's Ocean National Bank, and in November of that year unknown safe-crackers took $500,000 from the Boylston Bank in Boston.

□ On January 25, 1876, Eddie Goodie—"one of the smartest thieves in America, a man of wonderful audacity and resources," in Inspector Byrnes' description—led a gang that took $720,000 from the safe of the Northampton National Bank in Northampton, Massachusetts.

Although the professional thieves of this era did not belong to any "syndicate" or national organization, they did form a loose fraternity of sorts, moving about from place to place in the United States and Canada, and to some extent England and the Continent, according to the season and the opportunities. Their specialized criminal argot, much of it still in use, contributed to that sense of shared identity.

More important, the new professional thieves came from similar ethnic backgrounds; most were born in England or in the United States of English (or occasionally German or Irish) descent and had grown up in respectable working-class or middle-class homes. Ordinary street criminals, by contrast, generally were drawn from the poverty-stricken ethnic groups that formed the bulk of late nineteenth-century immigration. G. W. Walling, Byrnes' superior as Superintendent of the New York City Police Department, observed that "All the sneaks, hypocrites and higher grade of criminals, when questioned upon the subject, almost invariably lay claims to be adherents of the Republican Party; while, on the other hand, criminals of the lower order —those who rob by violence and brute force—lay claim in no uncertain terms to being practical and energetic exponents of true Democratic principles."

Whether Democrats or Republicans, the number of "criminals of the lower order" increased steadily after the turn of the century, as the corrosive impact of urban life destroyed the informal social controls under which the new immigrants, mostly from peasant backgrounds, previously lived.

II

The level of crime has always been high in the United States; the trend has fluctuated. From the turn of the century until the early 1930s, the trend was unmistakably upward. Judging by the homicide rate, the only crime for which reasonably accurate long-term statistics are available, the first three decades of the twentieth century saw an explosive increase in violent crime. The rate of death by murder, which ran only slightly above 1 per 100,000 population in 1900, shot up to 5 per 100,000 in 1910, and 7 per 100,000 in 1920. Cleveland, whose population in 1920 was one-tenth the size of London's, had six times as many murders and seventeen times as many robberies; Chicago, with one-third of London's population, had twelve times as many murders and twenty-two times as many robberies. And that was *before* the Roaring Twenties; by 1933, the rate of death by murder had climbed to 9.7 per 100,000.

These were years of rampant violence in all its forms. The United States has the bloodiest labor history of any industrial nation, and the late nineteenth and early twentieth centuries constitute the bloodiest portion of that history. In Colorado, to pick one of a number of examples, a "Thirty Years' War" of strikes and violence reached a climax in 1913–14, when coal miners struck against the Colorado Fuel and Iron Company. During the first five weeks of the strike, there were thirty-eight armed skirmishes between strikers and the company's private army; eighteen people were killed. In April, 1914, there was a fifteen-hour battle between strikers and militiamen. The battle ended when the militiamen set fire to the strikers' tent city near Ludlow, Colorado; two mothers and eleven children suffocated to death in what came to be known as the "Black Hole of Ludlow."

The close of World War I touched off a new wave of violence. The insatiable demand for labor during the war years broke the social and economic fetters that had kept black Americans bound to the rural South almost as effectively as they had been during slavery. When the war was over, many blacks were unwilling to return to their old subordinate status, and many whites were determined to return them to it. The ingredients for racial violence were present, and in the "Red Summer" of 1919, as [the poet] James Weldon Johnson called it, there were approximately twenty-five racial conflicts. Some were expanded lynchings; others, brief clashes that were quickly dissipated.

Seven incidents involved race riots of major proportions: in Washington, D.C.; Chicago; Knoxville; Omaha; Charleston, South Carolina; Longview, Texas; and Phillips County, Arkansas. The Phillips County bloodshed grew out of white farmers' determination to destroy a newly created union of black sharecroppers; by the time it ended, five whites and at least fifty to sixty blacks had been killed.

Criminal violence associated with organized crime gave the 1920s their special flavor and made cities such as Chicago notorious throughout the world. Before then, gambling and vice syndicates, the mainstays of organized crime, were relatively free from violence—at least by latter-day standards. January 17, 1920, the day the Volstead Act [which provided for the enforcement of the Prohibition Amendment] went into effect, represents the great watershed in the history of organized crime in the United States. Prohibiting the manufacture and sale of alcoholic beverages opened up the vast, and extraordinarily profitable, illegal industry of bootlegging, which was racked with violence from the start. Hijacking someone else's liquor was the fastest and most profitable method of entering the new industry; those who got a start that way were quick to create their own armies, often formed by hiring off-duty (and sometimes on-duty) policemen to protect them against other would-be bootleggers. (In 1926, one Chicago bootlegging "firm" alone had 400 policemen on its payroll.) Established underworld leaders remained on the sidelines, in part because they were content with their existing illegal enterprises, and in good measure because they were reluctant to use murder as a routine business technique. And murder *was* routine: in his classic 1929 study of organized crime in Chicago, John Landesco required four and a half pages just to catalog the principal casualties in the various Chicago "beer wars."

Thus a new generation of Americans, born in this century, took over the leadership of organized crime. By the early or middle 1920s, the top bootleggers were men in their twenties—predominantly Italian- and Jewish-Ameri-

cans, in contrast to the Irish-Americans who had dominated the earlier gambling and vice syndicates—and
utterly ruthless, as well as enormously ambitious. The new
leaders used their ruthlessness, along with their bootlegging
profits, to move into gambling and labor racketeering and
to invest in restaurants, night clubs, politics, and a host of
other enterprises. They were not prepared to retire when
Prohibition ended; with their capital, organizational ability,
and nationwide contracts, they broadened their investments
and continued to maintain a disproportionate amount of
power within the American underworld.

Even so, the end of Prohibition marked another watershed in the history of American crime and violence. For a
quarter of a century, the United States, perhaps for the
first time in its history, enjoyed a period in which crime
rates were either stable or declining and in which fear of
crime was relatively low. The death rate from homicide
dropped by 50 percent between 1933 and the early '40s;
despite the FBI's highly publicized gun battles with John
Dillinger and other criminals, the rate of other serious
crimes (rape, robbery, assault, and burglary) declined by
one third. Crime rebounded somewhat from its artificial wartime low after the Japanese surrender. Nonetheless, the
crime rate remained well below the levels of the 1920s and
early '30s until the current crime wave got under way in
the early 1960s.

Several factors account for this unusual period of domestic tranquillity. Despite the poverty and mass unemployment of the 1930s—in good measure *because* of poverty and
mass unemployment—Americans felt that they were all in
the same boat; the severity of the Great Depression helped
create a sense of community. Passage of the Wagner Act,
recognizing trade unions' right to collective bargaining,
ended the nation's long history of labor violence. Other
New Deal social reforms, combined with Franklin D.
Roosevelt's eloquence, made previously excluded racial
and ethnic groups feel as though they had been incor-

porated into American society. And World War II forged an even greater sense of national unity and purpose.

Demographic changes also contributed to the low level of criminal violence. Mass immigration from eastern and southern Europe was cut off in the early 1920s, and the Depression temporarily halted the movements of blacks from the rural South to the urban North. As a result, the old cities of the East and Midwest enjoyed a respite from their traditional (and traditionally traumatic) task of helping newcomers adjust to city life. Between 1940 and 1950, moreover, the population aged fourteen to twenty-four—the group from which most criminals are drawn—actually declined in size as a result of the sharp decline in the birth rate during the 1920s and '30s. During the war years, most young men were in the armed forces; when they returned to civilian life, they were eager to get on with their careers or their studies.

The result was a profound change in Americans' expectations about crime and violence. When one looks at the whole history of violence in the United States, the historian Richard Hofstadter suggests, what is striking is less the record of violence itself than Americans' "extraordinary ability, in the face of that record, to persuade themselves that they are among the best-behaved and best-regulated of peoples." This general tendency to shrug off unpleasant memories turned into a real historical amnesia after World War II. Because domestic tranquillity appeared to be the norm, Americans who came of age during the 1940s and '50s were unaware of how violent and crime-ridden the United States had always been. Although they continued to romanticize violence in detective stories and Westerns, an entire generation became accustomed to peace in their daily lives.

To most Americans, therefore, the upsurge in criminal violence that began around 1960 appeared to be an aberration from the norm rather than a return to it. The increase can be explained, in part, by a new and extraordinary demographic change that occurred between 1960 and 1975: the population aged fourteen to twenty-four grew 63 percent, more than six times the increase in all other age groups combined. In 1960, fourteen- to twenty-four-year-olds accounted for 69 percent of all arrests for serious crimes, although they comprised only 15.1 percent of the population. Without any change in young people's propensity for crime, the increase in their numbers alone would have brought about a 40 to 50 percent increase in criminal violence between 1960 and 1975. In fact, the number of serious crimes increased more than 200 percent. The change in the age distribution of the population thus accounts for only 25 percent of the increase; the rest is due to the greater frequency with which members of every age group, but particularly the young, commit serious crimes.

One reason for this increased propensity toward crime is what might be termed "demographic overload": the growth in the fourteen- to twenty-four-year-old group was so enormous, relative to the growth of the adult population, that the conventional means of social control broke down. In each generation, adults must grapple with the problem of inducting the young into the norms and values of adult society; as Norman Ryder, a Princeton University demographer, puts it, "Society at large is faced perennially with an invasion of barbarians." The task of "civilizing" those "barbarians" may be welcomed (as it is in the typical commencement address) as a chance for society to renew itself with youthful idealism, to reinvigorate its tired ideas and institutions and bring them into line with changing conditions. But the task is fraught with peril as well—both for the youthful invaders and for the society that must absorb them.

The peril is particularly great when those who are supposed to be doing the socializing are unsure of their role —a familiar and poignant by-product of migration. When parents live on unfamiliar cultural terrain, the conflict between the generations becomes anything but benign; the process of acculturation breaks down, and children find themselves adrift in a cultural no man's land. This is why the crime rate has always been particularly high among the first generation to be born in this country. The Wickersham Commission [which undertook the first national crime survey of the United States], wrote in 1931, in terms that apply to contemporary migrants from Latin America, China, and the rural South, that immigrant parents "do not understand the American community, and are consequently at a disadvantage in dealing with their own children, who at least *think* they understand it, and know they know more about it than their parents."

The ordinary relationship between child and parents is reversed, with the child developing a sense of superiority to the parent and an unwillingness to take any guidance from people so obviously out of tune with their surroundings. [Wickersham Reports]

Social controls have been weakened, too, by the older generation's growing uncertainty about its own values. "The prime fact about modernity," Walter Lippmann wrote nearly fifty years ago in *A Preface to Morals*, "is that it not merely denies the central ideas of our forefathers but dissolves the disposition to believe in them." The rise of science and the triumph of modern technology shattered the traditional molds in which, for several millennia, people had lived out their lives, thus undermining the institutional and intellectual bases of their faith. "The dissolution of the ancestral order," in Lippman's phrase, has been going on ever since, "and much of our current controversy is between those who hope to stay the dissolution and those who would like to hasten it." The rate of change has accelerated since the end of World War II, and the dissolution of tradition now feeds on itself. It is not simply that ordinary people increasingly question the legitimacy of rules and customs they once considered sacred, or that previously oppressed minorities refuse to remain in their "place," but that those who make or administer the rules have lost faith in their own legitimacy.

This is the background against which the demographic explosion of the 1960s took place. One way of looking at the magnitude of the task of socialization is to compare the size of the invading army of fourteen- to twenty-four-year-olds with that of the adult population. The years from fourteen to twenty-four are particularly important because it is during adolescence and youth that rebellion commonly occurs. Except among some segments of the lower class, where parents often lose control of their youngsters at an earlier age, children tend to be sufficiently influenced by their parents during the first twelve or thirteen years of life so that rebellion is an individual, rather than societal, concern. And rebellion tends to end in the early or mid-twenties, when young people settle down to jobs and careers and marriage and parenthood.

For a long time, the invading army was small enough to be contained without undue strain; from 1890 to 1960, the population aged fourteen to twenty-four increased slowly —in all but two decades, more slowly than the population aged twenty-five to sixty-four, which provides the time, energy, and resources needed to induct the young into American society. Thus the ratio of young to old either declined (as it did in five decades) or held steady.

Despite this demographic stability (and notwithstanding the relatively flat trend of crime in general), juvenile delinquency increased dramatically during the 1950s as the effects of large-scale migration and urbanization began to be felt once again. Even so, no one was prepared for the demographic dislocation that was to follow. Between 1960 and 1970, the number of fourteen- to twenty-four-year-olds grew more than 50 percent; in absolute terms, the increase came to 13.8 million people, a larger increase in that age group than had occurred during the preceding seventy years combined. As a result, the ratio of youths to adults shot up by 39 percent—the first time the ratio had increased in seventy years.

Already attenuated by social and cultural changes, the traditional channels for the transmission of culture from one generation to another broke down from demographic overload. Hence the young increasingly turned to one another for guidance; the youth culture emerged as a major socializing force, taking over a large part of the burden traditionally carried by parents, teachers, clergymen, and other adults. That culture had been in the making for several decades. The disappearance of the family as a unit of production, together with the growth of near-universal high school education and the increase in college attendance, radically altered the institutional settings in which young people live their lives. Instead of being part of multi-age, multi-generational family and work groups, the young now spend almost all their time in segregated settings, having contact only with members of their own age group and adults in positions of formal authority.

Increasingly, therefore, adolescents and youths derive their values, tastes, and life styles from their peer group rather than from their elders. The inward-looking character of the youth culture draws added strength from the increased affluence of most of its members. Just three or four decades ago, young people's labor was needed to help support the family; it was taken for granted that adolescents would turn their earnings over to their parents. Now many families have enough income to permit their children to spend some of it on their own tastes, and when teenagers do work, the tacit assumption seems to be that they will spend their earnings on themselves. This change in the economic relationship between the generations is symbolized by the different payroll practices of the Civilian Conservation Corps of the 1930s and the Job Corps of the 1960s and '70s. The CCC deducted a small allowance for the young people it employed, automatically sending the bulk of the money home to the parents; the Job Corps, by contrast, turns the paychecks over to its enrollees, sending an allotment home only on their request.

The result is that the young now control a substantial portion of the nation's discretionary income, a fact that gives the youth culture a power it otherwise would not have.

Young people now "can back up their tastes with money,"
the sociologist James S. Coleman writes. "They can buy the
records they like and the clothes they like, can go to the
movies they like, can pay for underground newspapers if
they like. Their inward-lookingness need not be confined
to finding their popular heroes among youth, or to con-
formity with norms laid down to their peers; it can be expressed also by the power of their dollars."

The size of young people's discretionary spending has led
businessmen to direct much of their sales effort at the
youth market; this, in turn, has increased young people's
"need" for more and more discretionary income. Indeed,
"keeping up with the Joneses" sometimes seems to be a
characteristic of the young even more than of the old;
certainly, peer pressures are far more intense among adolescents than among any other age group, and a teenager's
status often depends on the ability to buy the "right"
records and wear the "right" clothes. The adolescent need
for money, combined with the weakening of adult social
controls, has provided a lethal crimogenic force.

The pressure appears to be easing now. After a 10 percent increase in numbers during the first half of the decade,
the fourteen- to twenty-four-year-old population will grow
a scant 1.5 percent in this half-decade and then will decline by 6.6 percent over the next five years. The crime
rate seems to have stabilized, and criminologists have
begun to express cautious optimism about the outlook for
the 1980s.

Optimism may be premature. Among the groups most
heavily involved in street crime, the demographic trends
are less favorable than they are in the population as a whole.
Although the birth rate has been declining in every segment of American society, it nonetheless is considerably
higher among the poor than the non-poor; as a result the
age distribution of the poverty population lags behind that
of the rest of the population by a decade or more. In 1976,
only 24.1 percent of American males were below the age of
fourteen. Among the population officially classified as poor,

on the other hand, 39.7 percent were under fourteen years of age; and among poor black males, no fewer than 48.3 percent were in that age group. (The proportions were even higher among poor Puerto Ricans and Mexican-Americans.) In short, although the total number of fourteen- to twenty-four-year-olds is declining, the number of *poor* fourteen- to twenty-four-year-olds will continue to grow, and grow rapidly, for at least another decade. And the most rapid growth of all will occur in urban slums and ghettos, where criminal violence has always been concentrated.

III. INSTITUTIONAL CRIME

EDITOR'S INTRODUCTION

The FBI's crime index, concerned with what many call "street crimes," virtually ignores many crimes against businesses and by businesses. It also does not reflect those activities that organized criminals engage in, such as selling stolen property or drugs.

It is useful to consider street crime separately from institutional crimes, but it is also useful—and necessary—to examine white-collar crime and organized crime in detail. This sort of crime is "institutional" because it is so closely intertwined with American institutions such as the corporation and the government, without which it could not exist on its present large scale.

The criminologist Edwin H. Sutherland first used the term "white-collar crime" in 1941 to describe crime committed in the workaday world by people from the upper social and economic classes. Such crime has also been called "upperworld crime," to distinguish it from the "underworld" crimes of gangsters who satisfy demands for illicit drugs and high-risk loans, among other things.

This section opens with a *U.S. News & World Report* article on a crime wave that is sweeping American businesses. Next, Marc Leepson, a staff writer for *Editorial Research Reports,* looks into the growing problem of computer crime—a phenomenon undreamed of a generation ago because it was made possible only recently by a technological advance.

Next, an article in *Business Week* on business use of the lie detector—a device of questionable accuracy—reminds us that crime is not just a threat to individual Americans; it can be a test of the nation's ideals, as well.

Businesses can be victimizers as well as victims, as consumer advocates Ralph Nader and Mark Green illustrate in the fourth selection. They suggest stiff penalties for companies and those who run them as a way to make corporate crime less attractive and less rewarding.

The final two pieces in this section discuss organized crime—a provider of illicit services for millions of Americans. Francis A. J. Ianni, an anthropologist who has written several books on organized crime, views it as a way up and out of the ghetto for a succession of ethnic groups. Ralph C. Thomas, III, a lawyer, describes the type of organized crime he studied in the construction industry. He shows just which institutions profit from the theft of heavy equipment, and how this form of organized theft is nurtured by the very industry it robs.

CRIME WAVE AGAINST BUSINESS[1]

Reprinted from *U.S. News & World Report*

American business, from the "mom and pop" stores to giant industrial firms, is caught in a soaring crime wave.

From inside and outside, criminals are draining off cash and goods at the unprecedented rate of almost 40 billion dollars a year.

That is almost $185 for every man, woman and child in the United States. It amounts to more than 17 per cent of total business income before taxes.

And the money drain is increasing. Business losses have climbed 75 per cent in the past five years, and the number of offenses has increased by 35 per cent, according to a study by the Economic Unit of *U.S. News & World Report*.

White-collar crime occurs in many forms, including bankruptcy fraud, bribery, kickbacks and payoffs, theft by computer, consumer fraud, illegal competition and deceptive practices, credit-card and check fraud, embezzlement

[1] Article entitled "A $40-Billion Crime Wave Swamps American Business." *U.S. News & World Report*. 82:47–48. F. 21, '77. Copyright 1977 U.S. News & World Report, Inc.

and pilferage, insurance fraud, securities theft and fraud, theft of trade secrets and counterfeiting of products.

Arson is a major problem, too. The National Fire Protection Association estimates that 212,750 cases of arson did 1.26 billion dollars in damage to businesses, homes, schools and churches in 1975—a 6.5 per cent increase over losses a year earlier.

Losses, Failures

No business seems safe from losses due to theft by customers and employes. The trail of crime leads from the delivery docks to the executive suites.

Two million cases of shoplifting and theft were reported by companies to police in 1975. But the real number of crimes might be twice as large. Many go undetected; others are never reported.

Security officials estimate that 9 per cent of all employes steal on a regular basis. The President's Commission on Crime says 20 per cent of manufacturers find that theft of tools, equipment and materials or products by employes is a major and mounting problem. The results can be devastating. For example:

□ Thirty per cent of all business failures each year are a direct result of internal theft, according to insurance statistics.

□ Fraud is a major factor in losses that led to the closing of about 100 banks during a 20-year period.

□ Many department stores, food and apparel concerns lose 50 per cent of their profits to unaccountable "inventory shrinkage" that is generally believed to be theft. One result: Some merchandise is marked up an additional 15 per cent, thereby passing the costs on to consumers.

Escalating Problem

The crimes against business are increasing at a rate of about 10 per cent a year. White-collar convictions have shot up by almost 100 per cent in the past four years. Embezzlement, once infrequent, has soared almost 70 per cent since 1971.

Stores and offices were burglarized more than 930,000 times in 1975, according to the FBI's uniform crime reports. The loss: at least 350 million dollars. And that does not include offenses not reported to authorities.

Retailers listed 546,000 cases of shoplifting in 1975. In a study of one New York City store, 500 shoppers—picked at random—were followed and closely observed. One in 12 was seen stealing.

Nationwide, robbers hit chain stores 24,064 times during 1975. Banks were held up 4,180 times, an increase of almost 20 per cent in one year.

Yet, much crime is hidden. It shows up in inventory shortages or bankruptcy court. Retailers, a favorite target, lose an estimated 7.3 billion dollars a year, according to the Economic Unit's study.

The National Retail Merchants Association reports that 45 per cent of the stolen goods ends up in the hands of crooked employes; 35 per cent is taken by shoplifters, and the rest is attributed to "accounting errors."

Food supermarkets, with sales of 143 billion dollars a year, report that 1 billion is lost by theft. That is almost half of the 2.13 billion in profits after taxes generated by the industry in 1975.

Why are retailers hit so hard by dishonest employes and shoplifters? Says Gordon L. Williams, of the National Retail Merchants Association: "Our commodities—cold cash and readily fenced goods—are just what the thieves are looking for."

Penny a Sale

Stealing often is simple. In a busy New York candy store, a clerk underrang every sale on the cash register by 1 cent and for 22 years took home $5 a day. A supermarket manager in Oklahoma City set up his own cash register at peak periods and in three months stole $75,000.

Thefts from hotels and motels . . . [were estimated at]

500 million dollars for 1976. The industry counts on 1 of
every 3 guests' stealing something. Towels, silverware and
anything with the establishment's insignia are favorite
items. In a recent year, 4,600 Bibles were lifted from New
York City hotel rooms. Professional criminals frequently
strip motel rooms of TV sets, and corridors of ice-making
machines.

More than 11,000 cases annually of bank embezzlement
and consumer-related fraud are recorded by federal authorities. Crimes run from theft of cash by bank tellers to
fraudulent loans, involving millions, by bank officers.

"White-Collar Crime," a publication of the U.S. Chamber of Commerce, notes: Bribes, kickbacks and payoffs
"occur in dealings between companies, in transactions between business and Government and in negotiations between labor and management. They can involve the janitor
or the corporation president."

Industry leaders estimate that 7 billion dollars is paid
out in bribes or payoffs every year to obtain or retain
business, cover up short deliveries or inferior products, influence legislation, or negotiate "sweetheart" contracts with
labor unions.

In one instance, an engineering firm received a contract
from a turnpike authority after agreeing to put a relative of
the authority's chairman on the payroll and to permit the
relative to acquire 50 per cent of the firm's stock.

Another example: A wholesale buyer of women's dresses
and coats for a large mail-order company exacted payoffs
by threatening manufacturers with sudden and disastrous
reductions in orders.

Payoff for Daring

One reason for the massive cost is that criminals often
are bold and ingenious, while management frequently is
unsuspecting. A private investigating agency in New York
has listed 415 ways that employes can steal from their employers.

The risk of getting caught and being sent to prison

often is slight. The FBI managed to get convictions in only 4,610 white-collar cases in a 12-month period during 1975-76 —an infinitesimal number compared with the scope and breadth of the problem.

Often, white-collar crime is viewed by businessmen as a normal practice. A survey conducted recently by the Opinion Research Corporation found that almost half of American business executives interviewed saw nothing wrong with bribing foreign officials to attract or retain contracts.

Moreover, a survey by University of Georgia Prof. Archie B. Carroll showed that three fifths of corporate executives thought that young business managers would commit unethical acts to exhibit loyalty to their superiors.

Businessmen show reluctance to prosecute their own employes. "In most cases, a resignation is politely requested," complains a New York investigator.

Light Sentences

"Most times, the punishment of the convicted corporate crooks is relatively light, if the economic consequences of their deeds are considered," says [former] FBI Director Clarence M. Kelley.

An independent study of 138 offenders shows that 37— or 27 per cent—stole or mismanaged an average of 21.6 million dollars. They received only fines, suspended sentences or probation. The remaining 101 defendants were given jail sentences averaging 2.8 years.

The offenders included attorneys, bankers, politicians, stockbrokers, labor-union officials, business executives and a federal judge. When it comes to burglary, shoplifting, robbery and theft, only 1 case in 20 is officially solved by convictions. Even then, many of those charged with offenses are permitted to plead guilty to lesser charges.

"Businessmen are woefully uninformed about business crime," says Wayne Hopkins, an expert on crime at the U.S. Chamber of Commerce. "Some naïve businessmen think that putting up a fence and hiring guards affords protection. Meanwhile, thieves are stealing the company blind internally."

Cheating on Insurance

Insurance companies are defrauded of an estimated 1.5 billion dollars a year.

The situation is so critical that 318 insurance firms have formed the Insurance Crime Prevention Institute, which helps local investigators to uncover insurance rackets.

A fraud ring broken up recently in Cumberland County, N.C., involved more than 70 people. Its purpose: to cheat companies by filing false claims for auto accidents. Many of the "accidents" reported were staged, while others never occurred. Some defendants testified that they were instructed to hit another car in the rear as it was attempting to make a turn.

All the occupants of a car that caused a crash, plus some who were never at the scene, made insurance claims—some backed by allegedly forged documents.

Manipulating company records was a trick tried by a team in the Philadelphia area. The collection manager for a freight company placed good, collectible accounts into a bad-account file. Then he turned the accounts over to a collection agency run by an accomplice who kept 30 per cent of the money collected. The ruse netted the pair about $170,000 in a month's time before they were caught.

"Lost" Secrets

There are ways to rob a company without dipping into the till, as a major chemical firm discovered. Recently, it "lost" secret chemical formulas and documents valued at 16 million dollars.

The "loss" was explained when a former staff engineer attempted to sell the information to competitors, who advised the owners. The thief was caught and punished with a sentence of two years' probation and a fine of $2,000.

Crime experts and law-enforcement officials see no letup in growing crime rates and crime costs.

As long as companies accept crime as a day-to-day cost of operation, judges continue to hand out mild sentences and police remain understaffed, they say, business will continue to be the goose that lays golden eggs for white-collar criminals.

COMPUTER CRIME[2]

The annals of crime are recording a new and growing type of criminal activity: crimes involving computers. Fraud, embezzlement, blackmail and other crimes committed by the manipulation or misuse of computers cost Americans more than $100-million a year, according to the U.S. Chamber of Commerce. "Today business and government are more vulnerable to white-collar crime through use of computers than they were ever before or probably ever will be in the future," according to Donn B. Parker, senior management systems consultant at SRI International (formerly Stanford Research Institute) in Menlo Park, Calif. Parker, an expert on computer fraud, said a basic reason for this vulnerability is "the lack of progress in recognizing the threat and taking protective action in a period of rapid transition from manual, paper-based business activities" to fully computerized systems.

There are other reasons why computer-related crime is on the increase. For one thing, the number of computers and persons who work with them is rising steadily. International Data Corp., a publishing and market research consulting firm with headquarters in Waltham, Mass., reported that 86,314 general-purpose computers were installed in American businesses as of Jan. 1, 1977. . . . The company also reported that 176,315 minicomputers—small, relatively inexpensive units—are in use. In addition, the U.S. government uses some 10,000 computers.

[2] From *Computer Crime*, by Marc Leepson, staff writer. *Editorial Research Reports.* v 1 no 1:3–13. Ja. 6, '78. Copyright 1978 by Congressional Quarterly Inc. Reprinted by permission.

Computers touch the daily lives of nearly all Americans. They are used in nearly all business and governmental functions that are particularly susceptible to monetary theft. They are used by banks, public utilities, consumer credit companies and by financial offices in large corporations and in state, local and federal governments. Along with this increasing use of computers is a parallel rise in the number of persons who work with the machines—operators, programers and technicians. SRI International estimated that 2,230,000 Americans worked directly with computers in 1975. The figure is believed to be substantially higher today.

In many organizations, management supervisors have only faint knowledge of computer operations. That fact, combined with the near impossibility of checking the extremely complicated computer operating procedures, makes computers infinitely more vulnerable to misuse than the manual paper-based systems they replaced. "It is almost universally conceded in the electronic data processing industry that . . . it is extremely difficult to detect acts of embezzlement, fraud or thievery in which computers . . . are used as the principal tools of crime," Thomas Whiteside wrote in a recent *New Yorker* magazine series on computer crime. For example, a bank teller with access to the bank's computer makes transactions that are fundamentally different from those that are written on paper. The ease of access to computers leaves virtually no trails for auditors or other investigators to follow.

Difficulty of Detection and Conviction

August Bequai, a criminal lawyer who served as chairman of a Federal Bar Association subcommittee on white-collar crime, told Editorial Research Reports that the chance of an electronic crime being discovered is only one in a hundred. "And the likelihood of being convicted of a computer crime is one in five hundred and of going to jail one in a thousand. The odds for avoiding a stiff sentence are even more favorable."

Bequai and others have pointed out that the criminal justice system was set up to deal mainly with crimes of violence. But most white-collar criminals, especially computer culprits, are middle-class citizens who typically have no past record of criminal activity. Some 40 statutes are used to prosecute computer crimes but none of these laws was written specifically to cover these crimes. That situation contributes to the difficulties of administering justice to computer criminals. . . .

Sabotage and Vandalism by Employees

The many types of computer crime fall into two broad categories: (1) vandalism and sabotage, and (2) theft, fraud and embezzlement. Vandals and saboteurs have physically attacked computers on several occasions and for varied reasons. Some attacks have been politically motivated; some have come for personal reasons. A good number of vandalism cases involve disgruntled employees who steal or destroy computer equipment and tapes. Unhappy employees have attacked company computers with shotguns, screwdrivers and gasoline bombs. Malicious workers have deliberately mislabeled, misfiled or erased computer tapes.

A computer operator for Yale Express System in New York City, for example, thought he was being worked too hard and took revenge by destroying billing information he was supposed to enter into the trucking company's computer. He destroyed some $2-million worth of bills. A small business on the West Coast was hit even harder. An unhappy employee programed the company's computer to destroy all accounts receivable six months after he quit his job. This left no record of who owed the company money. It placed a newspaper advertisement asking its customers to pay what they owed. When only a few responded, bankruptcy followed. . . .

It is even possible to commit a murder by computer. Such a crime can take place because computers are capable of controlling life-support systems in hospitals. If a hospital computer guiding a patient's life-support system is tampered with to function incorrectly, the result could be death for the patient. What worries law-enforcement authorities about computer crimes involving vandalism and sabotage is that no special knowledge of computers may be needed. "If technical expertise is lacking," Arthur R. Miller [author of *The Assault on Privacy*, 1971] wrote, "a match, or a hammer in the case of a disc or a data cell, will do the same job . . . in a minute or two."

Electronic Theft, Fraud and Embezzlement

There are many kinds of computer theft, including theft of data, services, property and financial theft. "Time-shared" systems, in which several companies make use of the same computer, offer a particularly tempting target for the theft of services. One of the soft spots in such systems occurs when computerized information moves from the central processing unit through communications links to customers. In addition to the relatively simple task of bugging the transmission line and recording the electronic communications passing over it, the wiretapper might attach his or her own computer terminal to the line and join the group sharing the system's services. A bookmaker was caught using a college computer in this manner to run an illegal bet-taking operation.

One of the most publicized cases of computer-abetted property theft occurred in Los Angeles. Jerry Neal Schneider masterminded a scheme which resulted in his conviction for stealing an estimated $1-million worth of telephone equipment from the Pacific Telephone & Telegraph Co. in 1970-1972. Schneider accomplished what author Gerald McKnight called "one of the most amazing robberies in the history of crime" by using stolen computer information to order equipment through the Los Angeles telephone company's own computer. Before he was discovered, Schneider employed 10 persons to gather and sell the pirated equipment.

Confidential business information attracts thieves because it is likely to be very valuable. Large volumes of paper material can be boiled down and stored on small reels of magnetic tape, making it comparatively easy to steal. Thieves stole two reels of Bank of America tape at the Los Angeles International Airport in 1971 and threatened to destroy them if the bank did not pay a large ransom. In January 1976, the head programer of the computer department of Imperial Chemical Industries in Rotterdam, the Netherlands, took all the company's computer tapes that dealt with European operations. He asked for the equivalent of $200,000 in cash for their return.

Computer theft also lends itself to blackmail. Persons with access to computers have retrieved private data and threatened to make the information public. Such potentially damaging information includes poor college performance, erratic employment history, crime conviction or mental hospitalization. In one case, computer-room employees in Manchester, England, threatened to destroy their company's records if it did not give large salary increases.

The most costly, and perhaps the most common, computer crimes involve fraud and embezzlement. There are many cases of clerks with knowledge of their company's computers who have transferred money from customer accounts to their own pockets. But computer fraud does not always involve company clerks or bank tellers or persons working in computer rooms. Some schemes involve perpetrators with no access to computers or computer terminals. One such fraud has taken place in several major cities across the country.

It works like this: The criminal opens a small checking account in a bank and then steals some blank checking deposit slips—the ones that banks provide for depositors who do not have premarked checking deposit forms. The criminal takes the blank forms to an unscrupulous printer who adds the criminal's magnetic-ink checking account number to all the slips. The doctored deposit forms are slipped back into their usual place at the bank. Everyone using them is therefore depositing money into the criminal's checking account. Within days, hundreds of thousands of

dollars are sent by the bank's computer into the perpetrator's account. The thief withdraws the money and
moves on.

By far the biggest computer-related crime on record
involved a nationwide investment firm, the Equity Funding Corporation of America. The Equity Funding scandal
first came to public attention in 1973. Computer crime was
but one part of a widespread illegal financial fraud masterminded by the highest officers of the now-bankrupt company. Equity's president and 21 other executives were convicted in 1975 of setting up life insurance policies for some
56,000 fictitious persons and selling the policies to other
insurance companies. The bogus insurance policies existed
only inside Equity Funding's computer. A bankruptcy
trustee's report calculated that the total value of the
fraudulent policies was $2.1-billion.

Computer fraud is by no means relegated to private
enterprise. The federal government, too, has been the victim
of computer crime. The General Accounting Office, Congress's investigating arm, reported in 1976 on 69 instances of
improper use of computers in the U.S. government. The
69 cases resulted in losses of some $2-million. The report
said that the 69 cases "do not represent all the computer
crimes involving the federal government since agencies do
not customarily differentiate between computer-related and
other crimes." The GAO investigation further revealed the
distinct possibility that a large number of computer crimes
in the federal government have yet to be detected or reported. Computer-related crimes were documented at all
levels of the government.

In one case, an Internal Revenue Service programer fed
information into an IRS computer to funnel unclaimed tax
credits into a relative's account. Another IRS programer
used a computer to take checks being held for those whose
mailing addresses could not be located and deposit the
checks into his own account. Concern about the vulner-
ability of the federal government's computers is high be-

cause the government pays tens of billions of dollars by computer every year. The crimes documented by the GAO ranged from those involving hundreds of dollars to those involving hundreds of thousands of dollars. . . .

Efforts to Improve Safeguards, Training

This is not to say, though, that computer supervisors are not aware of security problems and are doing nothing about it. The Federal Bureau of Investigation recently opened a special course at its Quantico, Va., training center to train FBI agents and state and local police for investigating consumer fraud and other white-collar crimes. But the course has come in for criticism. Thomas Whiteside wrote: ". . . [A]ccording to commercial computer-security people I have talked with, the training so far offered is not of a very advanced type in relation to all the ramifications of the existing criminal problem." August Bequai said of the FBI training program: "It's not enough to train a person on what a computer can do. You have to train him in the sophisticated and complicated frauds that a complex computer is capable of performing."

International Business Machines, the leading manufacturer of computers, recently came up with recommendations to prevent computer crime. IBM studied computer security for several years and is reported to have spent $40-million on the effort. The company recommends four basic measures to help prevent computer abuse: (1) rigid physical security, (2) new identification procedures for keyboard operators, (3) new internal auditing procedures to keep a fuller record of each computer transaction, and (4) new cryptographic symbols to scramble information. Even with those and other precautions, security problems remain. "The data security job will never be done—after all, there will never be a bank that absolutely can't be robbed," IBM's director of data security, John Rankine, has said. . . .

BUSINESS BUYS THE LIE DETECTOR[3]

"We have resisted it," says Charles S. Thompson, president of Thoreson Sales Co., a Dallas toy and sporting goods wholesaler. "I don't like it now, but it's about the only tool left." He is talking about polygraph, or lie-detector, testing, which Thoreson has now begun to require of its employees. Thompson's reluctance to use the machines reflects the unease about such practices inside and outside American businesses. But his decision to go ahead is in line with the growth of such testing throughout the business world.

According to a survey conducted by researchers John Belt and Peter Holden of Wichita State University, fully one-fifth of the nation's largest companies, engaged in a wide range of business pursuits, now use lie detectors. Operators of the machines report that as much as 90 per cent of their business now comes from corporate clients, and in many cases their volume has doubled within the past five years. In 1958 only seven companies offered lie-detector testing by listing themselves in the Manhattan Yellow Pages. By 1968 their number had grown to 17, and today [1978] it is 31.

A *Business Week* survey confirms that companies large and small, in all parts of the U.S., have turned to lie detectors, including the controversial new voice-stress analyzers that purport to measure changes in inaudible microtremors of the human voice. Whereas retailers have been the traditional users of such machines, the survey shows that lie detectors are now used by nearly every type of company.

□ Jack Eckerd Corp., of Clearwater, Fla., will spend $500,000 this year to polygraph employees in its 16-state, 800-unit chain of Eckerd Drugs outlets. At some time in his or her employment, everyone in the company, including the president, must take the test.

[3] Article in *Business Week*. p 100–1+. F. 6, '78. Reprinted from the February 6, 1978, issue of *Business Week* by special permission. © 1978 by McGraw-Hill, Inc., New York, N.Y. 10020. All rights reserved.

□ In Maryland, a manufacturer was so eager to reduce theft that it offered employees a profit-sharing plan in return for their submission to Psychological Stress Evaluator (a type of voice analyzer) tests. The workers accepted.

□ Kemper Corp. is using PSES in Massachusetts to test tape recordings it routinely makes of auto insurance claims. In about 20 per cent of the tests, which are conducted on "suspicious" claims and usually without the claimants' knowledge, the analyzers have detected stress that led to further investigation and sufficient evidence to deny a fraudulent claim.

□ An Atlanta nursing home uses polygraphs to screen out potentially sadistic or disturbed nurses and orderlies.

□ Despite their official and often vehement opposition to the use of lie detectors in the workplace, national labor unions have had recourse to them for their internal investigations, as well as to verify complaints from members who have been fired. Five Midwestern polygraph operators contacted by *Business Week* say they conducted 32 separate investigations for union locals between 1960 and 1971.

While the popularity of lie detection is growing, so is the probability that the government will ultimately restrict business use of such machines. No federal law now specifically applies, but a commission set up under the Privacy Act of 1974 recommended a prohibition. The Equal Employment Opportunity Commission has studied the machines and could, under its broad mandate, curtail lie-detector use.

Restrictions Ahead?

Congress, too, may step in. Indiana Democrat Birch Bayh's Senate subcommittee on the Constitution recently held a round of hearings on his proposed bill to limit lie-detector testing. "The vast growth of technology makes the availability of invading privacy so real that it seems time for Congress to consider the matter," says Senator Bayh, who has planned more hearings this spring.

Not all employers who have used lie detectors are con-

vinced that they work, and many have shunned them because of their adverse effect on employee morale. But the
majority are satisfied customers, and a significant number
contend that workers actually are pleased at the chance
to show they are honest. Perhaps most important, lie detectors are quicker and cheaper than background checks or
full investigations.

Certainly businessmen have cause to seek remedies for
worker theft and other forms of dishonesty. According to
the National Retail Merchants Assn., employees of member companies steal as much as $40 billion in goods from
their employers each year.

"The average merchant doesn't recognize that he loses
more to employees than to others," says a spokesman for
Montgomery Ward & Co., a user of lie detectors. "From
50 per cent to 70 per cent of our loss goes to employees,
and this is the same for any retailer. Shoplifters don't take
you for nearly as much."

Widespread Problem

But retailers are not the only businessmen to have felt
the bite of employee theft. In a manual entitled *Profit-
ability Through Loss Control,* bank security officers Bill I.
Ehrstine and Jack A. Mack point out that nearly one-third
of the 1,500 U.S. businesses that go bankrupt each year do
so because of dishonest workers.

Many employers who use lie detectors claim they are
doing so because other avenues of investigation are denied
them. "It seems as if the more laws are passed, the more
chance the deadbeats and criminals have," says Ehrstine,
whose employer, the Third National Bank & Trust Co. of
Dayton, Ohio, polygraphs "satellite" workers such as clean-
ing crews and guards. John S. Ammarell Jr., executive vice-
president of Wackenhut Corp., one of the country's largest
security agencies, says employers have grown leery of passing
along too much information about former employees who
apply elsewhere.

"The information," he says, "is usually very sketchy because they're afraid of being sued. Invasion, right of privacy, and fair-credit reporting have scared the hell out of employers. And some states forbid disclosure of arrest and conviction records."

Others fault the low moral tone of the times for the spread of lie detectors. "Let's face it," says M. Warren Seymour, a former agent of the Federal Bureau of Investigation and now president of Counterintelligence Services, Inc., of Warwick, R.I., "taking home trinkets is part of the job for retail employees."

Ardent foes of lie detectors, such as David T. Lykken, a professor of psychiatry and psychology at the University of Minnesota, say that lie detectors victimize workers more often than not, and that employers would be better advised to create an atmosphere of honesty. According to Lincoln M. Zonn, president of a national polygraph service, half of all internal theft is due to sheer laxity on management's part. "They just aren't controlling things properly by systems and procedures," asserts Zonn.

Many Uses

Whatever their problems or stated objectives, U.S. businesses have found a surprising range of applications for lie detectors. Not only are they looking for thieves, junkies, liars, alcoholics, and psychotics among their workers; increasingly, the machines are being used to screen out applicants with health problems without resort to more expensive physical exams. According to Bill R. Cannon, owner of a security agency in Dallas, Tex., his customers want polygraphs to reveal if a job seeker has a history of filing too many workmen's compensation claims.

In addition, some employers want to spot workers who do not intend to stay on the job long enough to warrant costly training programs. Others are clearly interested in learning whether an interviewee holds extreme political opinions. Some have been known to wonder about unusual sex habits. Most agree that such questions are difficult if not impossible to pose through written questionnaires, or are illegal to ask at all.

Cutting Losses

However, the overriding concern of most lie-detector users is to cut losses through employee theft. San Francisco-based Foremost-McKesson Inc., for instance, has been polygraphing workers in its 100 wholesale drug and liquor warehouses across the U.S. for 25 years. Before beginning the policy, says Richard D. Paterson, Foremost's director of security, the company was plagued by theft rings. He notes that a review in the late 1960s concluded that Foremost-McKesson had achieved a fourfold reduction in thefts. "[Theft] has become unusual for us," he says.

The manager of a Long Island housewares outlet feels that the use of polygraphs has made the difference between success or failure in his low-margin business. And at Atlanta-based Munford Inc., which operates more than 1,000 food stores, as well as warehouses and import stores, polygraph tests are credited with saving millions of dollars. Munford, which conducts 25,000 polygraph exams each year, has sold its stores in states where the practice is prohibited.

On the other hand, many companies make only selective use of lie detectors. At Aluminum Co. of America, polygraphs are used sparingly for in-house investigations. Interviewees must grant written permission to the company, sign a consent form, and must give the examiner a written O.K., too. Initially, Standard Oil Co. (Ohio) had decidedly more enthusiasm for lie detectors than it has today, and it has stopped using a voice analyzer. Testing has dropped from a high of 50 exams per year to just a few.

Punishment

Just as their policies toward lie detection itself vary, so do company procedures when an employee is caught. A California company, seeking to learn the cause of shrinkage in its shoe warehouse, polygraphed the building's dozen workers. All flunked, and some were fired. But at another company on the West Coast, a vice-president was permitted to resign after confessing during a voice-analyzer exam to chiseling on his expense account and stealing from the company. The confession was kept secret from his new employers. A company in New England set up a repayment schedule for an employee who, after a lie-detector exam, confessed to stealing $22,000. As added insurance that he will pay up, the company has taken a lien on his mortgage.

One thing that many businessmen do not seem to have taken into account is that lie detectors are only as good as the people who conduct the tests, and that employers victimize themselves as well as workers when testing is slipshod. Many polygraph operators contend that their clients shop price before accuracy, an attitude that opens the door to abuse. "I've come to the conclusion that polygraphs and similar equipment are only investigative crutches," says the security officer for an oil company. "We're better off depending on gathering evidence and direct confrontation with suspects and building a case that way."

CRIME BY BUSINESSES[4]

As defined by sociologist Edwin Sutherland in the late 1940s, white collar crime is committed by businessmen, government officials and professionals in their occupational roles. The culprits look like respectable citizens, not shifty-eyed mobsters, which makes it so hard for many to accept what they do as "crime." White collar crime has never made it into Richard Nixon's "law and order" lexicon.

Even more difficult to establish is *corporate crime*, involving premeditated business predations. Sutherland found

[4] From an article entitled "Crime in the Suites," by Ralph Nader, consumer advocate and founder of the Project for Corporate Responsibility, and Mark Green, former director of Corporate Accountability Research Group and co-editor (with Ralph Nader) of *Corporate Power in America. The New Republic.* 166:17–21. Ap. 29, '72. Reprinted by permission of *The New Republic.* © 1972, The New Republic, Inc.

that slightly over 97 percent of the corporations studied were "recidivists," with at least two convictions each. He concluded that "practically all large corporations engage in illegal restraint of trade, and . . . from half to three-fourths of them engage in such practices so continuously that they may properly be called 'habitual criminals.' "

In 1961 the *Harvard Business Review* surveyed its subscribers on the issue of business ethics. About four out of seven respondents to one question believed that businessmen "would violate a code of ethics whenever they thought they could avoid detection." When asked, "In your industry, are there any [accepted business] practices which you regard as unethical?" four-fifths responded affirmatively. That same year, a General Electric executive sentenced to jail for conspiring to fix prices asserted, "Sure collusion was illegal, but it wasn't unethical."

But what's unethical often *is* illegal. Take antitrust crime, the sabotage of economic competition. Antitrust offenses include price-fixing, market divisions, and exclusionary boycotts—all of which result in inflated consumer prices, inflated corporate returns and often rewarded inefficiencies. The possible penalties according to the Sherman Antitrust Act: up to a year in jail and/or a $50,000 fine per violation.

Although the number of criminal antitrust cases prosecuted each year by the Justice Department is small (due largely to their meager resources)—averaging 25 a year from 1960 to 1964, and 11 a year from 1965 to 1970—the total number of industries involved in criminal antitrust acts in the past 30 years is quite large. Nearly every conceivable industry has been affected, from milk and bread to heavy electrical equipment, from lobster fishing and the cranberry industry to steel sheets and plumbing fixtures. This large volume, plus the fact that the industries implicated are in no significant way unlike others, lead some analysts to conclude that their illegal acts are practiced elsewhere—without detection.

The vast scale of the electrical manufacturing conspiracy of 1961, involving nearly every firm in that industry, startled many complacent antitrust watchers who had intoned that price-fixing was nonexistent, even unnecessary, in an oligopolistic industry. The comment by a defendant in that case, that "conspiracy is just as much 'a way of life' in other fields as it was in electrical equipment," made observers wonder how many other industries were price-rigged. Our antitrust study *The Closed Enterprise System* asked the presidents of *Fortune*'s top 1,000 firms how many agreed with this assertion. Nearly *60 percent* of those answering (100) concurred that "many . . . price-fix." And the only scholarly attempt to estimate the extent of price-fixing concluded in the *Northwestern Law Review* that "it is apparent that price fixing is quite prevalent in American business."

While antitrust crime may seem only remotely relevant —esoterica to be unraveled by economists but surely not consumers—its impact on corporations and the public is direct and vast. An international quinine cartel cornered the world market in the early sixties, raising the price of quinine from 37¢ an ounce to $2.13, and thereby pricing it beyond the means of patients who needed it to restore natural heart rhythm. "I cannot continue to pay these high prices for quinine," complained one elder citizen to a Senate subcommittee, "yet my doctor tells me I cannot live without it." Between 1953 and 1961, 100 tablets of the antibiotic tetracycline cost as little as $1.52 to manufacture but retailed for about $51; ten years later, after congressional hearings and a criminal indictment exposed a conspiracy among some of the nation's largest drug houses, the retail price for the same quantity was approximately $5. While the average American paid about 20¢ for a loaf of bread in 1964, the Seattle consumer was paying 24¢, or 20 percent more, due to a local price-fixing conspiracy, which was finally ended by a Federal Trade Commission ruling; it was estimated that consumers in the Seattle area were overcharged by $35 million. The electrical price-fixing cases of 1961 saw seven corporate officials sent to jail (20 others got suspended sentences). Seven billion dollars of equipment sales were implicated during the conspiracy, and more money was stolen by this one suite crime than all the street crime for that year combined. Summarized one unindicted official, "the boys could resist everything but temptation." Or as Woody Guthrie sang in "Pretty Boy Floyd," . . . [some men rob with guns and others rob with fountain pens].

What are the countervailing costs which could dissuade such business crime? There are four basic sanctions—imprisonment, criminal fines, treble damages and loss of good will. Yet cushioning their sting is an effective combination of official impediments: the pattern of Justice Department enforcement, the frequent settlement of criminal cases by so-called "no-contest pleas," and general judicial hostility. . . .

A combination of new measures should ease antitrust crimes into extinction. All are predicated on an obvious fact about this genre of crime: violations are neither spontaneous nor *ad hoc,* but are carefully planned out by intelligent people balancing risks and benefits; it is with just such calculating individuals that strong penalties can be successful deterrents.

The long-standing judicial failure to impose penal and monetary sanctions compels the need for minimum penalties. When a defendant admits to or is found guilty of a knowing and willful violation, there should be a minimum prison term of four months for the first offense and one year for the second. A minimum fine of one percent of the corporation's sales receipts for the years of the conspiracy (subsidiaries taken separately) would help make the punishment fit the crime. Within the judge's discretion, it could go up to 10 percent. Since it has been estimated that a price fixing conspiracy can, on the average, inflate prices by 25 percent, it does not seem unreasonable to insist that convicted firms divest themselves of at least a minimal portion of their illegally acquired proceeds. With serious financial penalties built into the fabric of enforcement, the profit motive itself should be adequate incentive to self-regulate the system into compliance.

Just as the Landrum-Griffin Act ousts labor leaders from their positions for criminal convictions, any member of management who obtains a criminal record relating to his corporate duties should take a permanent vacation. So that individuals not be relieved of the bite of liability for their personal wrongs, federal law should forbid the corporate indemnification of criminal, individual fines—which is permitted by some states today. A corporate agent in a supervisory capacity should be held criminally liable if he has specific knowledge of an antitrust violation within his area of supervision, and if he willfully fails to report or end it; the intentional disregard of a duty should entail legal accountability. Also, corporations should be compelled to inform the public of their criminal convictions—as suggested by the National Commission on the Reform of Federal Criminal Laws—as the only way to counteract massive publicity which projects them as concerned and magnanimous citizens.

Finally, corporations should voluntarily stop putting impossible demands and pressures on middle rank executives, the kind which can only compel them to fix prices in order to reach projected profit margins. What did lead John H. Chiles—a division manager at Westinghouse, 57 years old, a senior warden of his local Episcopal church, vice president of his United Fund drive, and according to his lawyer, "the benefactor of charities for crippled children and cancer victims"—to meet illegally with his competition? No doubt there was a breakdown of personal morality, but, as Chiles's lawyer also argued, "There is such a thing as business compulsion . . . there is such a thing as atmosphere; there is such a thing as knowing acquiescence in a situation." The top executives in the electrical firms were never indicted or convicted. Instead, just two months before sentencing of his subordinates began, chairman Ralph

Cordiner was selected as the National Association of Manufacturers' man of the year.

SOCIAL BANDITRY AND A BLACK MAFIA[5]

Why are blacks and Puerto Ricans sympathetic to, and even envious of, the blacks and Puerto Ricans who have achieved success in organized crime? First of all, organized crime is accurately viewed by them in many ways as merely one end of the American business and industrial structure and, as such, is viewed more as a business venture than as a moral evil. Although organized crime is an illicit enterprise, it follows many of the same rules as the American business system. Ghetto dwellers view organized crime from the same perspective many Americans adopt when they regard the American system of business enterprise. That is, they envy it and criticize it at the same time. The line between sharp business practice or successful political machination and crime is thin and can scarcely be distinguished by many Americans.

It is poverty and powerlessness that provide the moral climate leading to acceptance of organized criminal activities in the ghetto. Like most Americans living in our consumer society, ghetto dwellers are hungry for money and for the goods and services it can procure. They have accepted the American achievement model of striving for success and security. Yet they are cut off from many legitimate ways of obtaining financial security, and, at the same time, they have fewer ways than white Americans to achieve the psychological security that can reduce the incidence of crime. When a man is financially secure, is happy and secure in his work, has a stable family life and lives in a stable community, he has little reason to consider criminal activity as a vocational possibility. But blacks and Puerto Ricans

[5] From *Black Mafia: Ethnic Succession in Organized Crime*, by Francis A. J. Ianni, anthropologist. Simon & Schuster. '74. p 322–8. Copyright 1974 by Francis A. J. Ianni. Reprinted by permission of Simon & Schuster, Inc.

like other ethnics before them see organized crime as one of the few routes to success, to financial and thus psychological security, open to them. In every society, criminals tend to develop when social conditions seem to offer no other way of escaping bondage. Poverty and powerlessness are at the root of both community acceptance of organized crime and recruitment into its networks. Conditions of poverty also nurture community desires for the services organized criminal operations provide. Escapism accounts in part for both widespread drug use and numbers gambling; the resentment poverty and powerlessness bring in the subordinated population makes drugs and gambling attractive as mechanisms of rebellion. Organized crime is esteemed for the very reason that society outlaws it.

It is important to note in . . . [the] context of ethnic succession that none of these characteristics of or attitudes toward organized crime is culture-bound: the structures of poverty and powerlessness, rather than the structures of the black and Puerto Rican cultures, seem most responsible. It is probable that certain subcultures are more prone to certain kinds of specific behavior as a result of the normative structure of those cultures. . . . Among the Italian-Americans, for example, the cultural model provided by Mafia and other secret criminal organizations in southern Italy led to a high degree of organizational development in the criminal syndicates operating in the United States. Certainly if there is a movement toward higher organization within black and Puerto Rican networks, this movement will respond to the culture imperatives of those groups. This, however, is very different from a cultural propensity toward organized crime. Organized crime involves a calculated pattern of offense to one or more of a culture's norms. Its presence is perhaps predictable whenever one culture in a dominating way holds such norms over the heads of a lively and energetic dominated subculture. In such a situation, organized crime will probably persist until an adequate degree of assimilation and accommodation takes place. In effect I am suggesting that

organized crime results from a conflict of cultures and I am
further hypothesizing that organized crime as we know it in
the United States requires an underclass of minority status
ethnics in order to be operative.

There seems to be little question that assimilation and
accommodation with the larger American societies are the
chief aims of black and Puerto Rican organized crime
activists. This is not to suggest that they are not criminals
and that they are not involved in illegal activities but
rather that, as was true of the Italians, the Jews and the
Irish before them, the greater motivation is to achieve
social, occupational and residential mobility. Even while
they themselves might never articulate such aims, even
when their goals are limited by the scope of their own
neighborhood, nevertheless they still exhibit single-minded
striving for the material wealth and social security that mo-
tivates others in society as well. If . . . [they] cannot themselves quite imagine movement toward respectability and
security, then certainly they want this for their children
and their children's children.

Another source of militancy in crime is the prison,
where . . . [observers find] the predominantly black inmate
population is becoming increasingly politicized—not only
in search of improved prison conditions but against racist
social conditions outside the walls as well. This growing
protest is marked by a good deal of self-education in political and revolutionary literature, black-history study groups
and a new sense of identity as blacks. Thus, in the prisons,
where institutional racism brings blacks together in the
courts, the lessons of the street are reinforced and the crime
activist-become-revolutionary is a growing pattern. As often
happens, the image becomes part of the popular culture as
well and the new cinema crime heroes—*Shaft, Superfly* and
a growing host of others—are as militantly black as they are
violently criminal.

Then there are the black revolutionaries themselves;
groups ranging from the Muslims and Panthers to the Black
Liberation Army are becoming increasingly paramilitary in

structure and in the use of uniforms and arms as well as in their aims. Drawn from the same ghetto street society as the black crime activists, they are also the frequent targets of police harassment and often view themselves as essentially defense organizations against white oppression and open hostility. It is not too improbable to imagine that whether on the streets or in the prisons, there will be increasing contact between militant crime activists and revolutionaries. This becomes particularly probable when one assumes, as we must, that unlike previous generations of immigrants who used organized crime as a means of escaping the slum and gaining some access to social mobility, blacks will very probably not be permitted to take that route. Cut off from the "normal" process of transition into the legitimate world, black organized crime activists could become increasingly militant and even revolutionary and the vast sums that accrue from organized crime could be diverted to financing liberation movements. . . .

Eventually, all these factors could serve to bring together the presently scattered black organized crime networks into a classical Mafia. Eric J. Hobsbawm, the eminent British social historian, has studied Mafia not as a specific organization but as a universal code of behavior that develops in societies lacking a strong social order and in which an oppressed group within that society sees the authorities as wholly or partly hostile and unresponsive to their needs. He has described Mafia in Sicily and elsewhere as a form of *social banditry* that seeks to overcome oppression and poverty through collective rebellion against real or imagined oppressors, which in time develops into "an institutionalized system of a law outside the official law." While Hobsbawm was studying and so speaking primarily of peasant rebels who resort to social banditry as a reformist movement, the characteristics he cites are easily recognizable in the urban social banditry that could form among blacks. Mafia is, first and foremost, a form of social protest that can, like the classical Mafia in Sicily and its counterpart among the earlier Italian immigrants to the United States, use crime as a weapon of protest. This protest is expressed in a general attitude toward the law that tends to develop where that law is considered unresponsive or hostile and alien to the culture of the rebellious group, and so they develop their own code of rules to regulate and regularize relationships between and among themselves and in their relationship with the larger society. In this sense, Mafia becomes a network of gangs held together by a common code. Hobsbawm also points out that such "Mafias" tend to develop in societies where there is not an effective social order and where Mafia provides a parallel machine of law and organized power that in time, so far as the people in the areas under its influence are concerned, becomes the only effective law and power. Each of these conditions exists in black ghettos today, and the coalescence of the presently scattered networks into a black Mafia held together by a rudimentary ideology of black power is a distinct possibility within this decade. The emerging militancy of the black Mafia may provide an even more cohesive organizing principle for blacks than kinship was for the Italians and may well develop into a revolutionary social movement by joining with other militant aspirations and groups. Kinship-based clannishness comes out of a rural primitive tradition of bonding that cannot resist the social forces of the city and cannot support it. Militancy, however, does have an urban base, and while social and economic mobility of Italians destroyed the "family structure," the resistance to such mobility on the part of blacks will serve to reinforce their militant base in the ghetto. The new black mafioso will, in fact, be an urban social bandit.

Finally, there is the condition of better access to political power and the ability to corrupt it as a prior factor in the elaboration and extension of black organized crime outside the confines of the ghetto. The evidence here is more difficult to deal with because it is, to some extent, contradictory. On the one hand, it is well established in the social history of the city that ethnic groups succeed to power in politics as they do in crime and that the two forms of mobility are often connected. There is evidence that blacks are moving ahead in politics in the large urban areas just as they are in organized crime. What is less evident is that the necessary connections between politics and its corruptibility and black movement in organized crime will coincide. It is a maxim in the underworld that graft and corruption are color-blind and that the police and politicians will take graft regardless of the color of the hand that delivers it. It is difficult to imagine, however, that blacks will be able to insinuate themselves into the kinds of social relationships with white politicians that are the environment within which deals are made, bribes are offered or sought, and protection developed. Again, the black movement in both politics and crime, like so many other processes of social advancement among them, comes at a time when much of the power and profit has already been milked from the system by the groups that preceded them. The rampant corruption of our political system, reaching up to and including the White House, could raise the costs and risks of corruption to a prohibitive point. This already seems to be the case in New York City, where the revelations of . . . bribe taking by the police seem to have *doubled* the costs of bribery in just one year's time.

While the growth of a black Mafia is fairly well known or at least perceived in black and Puerto Rican neighborhoods, it would not be unfair to say that, aside from the occasional newspaper headlines, there is little public knowledge that it is going on. To judge from its actions, the greater society seems to consider black and Puerto Rican organized crime as one of the small prices it must pay for the continuance of the many psychological and economic comforts that accrue from the existence of an ethnic underclass. Indeed, when measured against the cost of eliminating such crime, the costs are small. The most visible cost—from the thefts and muggings of narcotics addicts—touch only a few people in the large urban areas. In many respects

there is also a continuation of that traditional attitude of
the criminal justice system: so long as ghetto dwellers keep
their crimes within the ghetto and do not spill outside,
leave them to themselves. It is when the muggings and the
robberies reach the non-ghetto areas that there is a strong
outcry. This attitude, which has traditionally been part of
our law enforcement value system, allows organized crime
to thrive within the ghetto. Once the organized crime networks find profitable sources of revenue outside the ghetto,
then the growing economic, political and social impact of
organized crime becomes a matter of public interest and
social policy. In the meantime, blacks and Hispanics must
continue to face the same basic dilemma that confounded
earlier generations of Irish, Jews and Italians: *How do you
escape poverty through socially approved routes when such
routes are closed off from the ghetto?* Crime resolves the
dilemma because it provides a quick if perilous route out.

ORGANIZED CRIME IN THE
CONSTRUCTION INDUSTRY[6]

The construction industry is the habitat of many species
of crime, which can be classified according to who commits
it—an employee, a vandal, an amateur thief, an ordinarily
honest citizen, or an organized crime ring.

The daily disappearance of tools, ranging from ham-
mers and screwdrivers to small compressors and power saws,
is so predictable that many contractors include the cost of
the loss in their job estimates. They are convinced that
much of this equipment is simply "walked off" the job by
their own workmen, who regard the material as "borrowed"
for use in their home workshop, to repair a machine, or on
a moonlighting job.

[6] Article by Ralph C. Thomas, III, lawyer. Reprinted with permission of the
National Council on Crime and Delinquency, from Ralph C. Thomas, III, "Organized Crime in the Construction Industry," *Crime & Delinquency*, July 1977,
pp. 304–311. © 1977 by the National Council on Crime and Delinquency.

There is evidence that the vandalism toll is also mounting. Windshields have been smashed, machines broken, and expensive tires punctured or slashed; holes have been punched in radiators; engines have been ruined by sand, dirt, and bits of metal thrown into critical working parts.

In the amateur theft, slightly more common than vandalism, a small and easily taken hand tool disappears while more expensive items are left behind.

Contractors assert that, if he is not watched carefully, the "law-abiding nice guy" who requests permission to "pick up scraps" will pick up any valuable construction material that is not nailed down. One contractor reported catching a little old lady helping herself to 4′ x 8′ sheets of ⅝″ plywood on a site where he was building a freeway. She had stacked five sheets in her pickup when he challenged her. "You shouldn't be upset about my taking this lumber," she snorted, "I'm a taxpayer!"

A greater concern of the contractors is the increase in the number of thefts of large, heavy equipment, such as big-wheeled compressors, earth movers, tractors, and even cranes and shovels. Offhand, it would seem that the size, cost, and highly specialized use of such items would make them readily detectable and suspect when offered at cut-rate prices to buyers. But there is evidence that this illicit trade is managed by organized crime rings, which have brought sophisticated techniques of theft to the construction industry. . . .

How the System Works

Mr. Willis slowly sipped his martini and tried to look as happy as the twenty other contractors who circulated throughout the bar. The Hyatt Regency Cocktail Lounge was one of the classiest in the Bay Area and Willis did have his image to consider. During the last few months, it had been extremely difficult for him to smile about anything. Three months ago a $45,000 bulldozer was stolen from one of his job sites. Then three waves of theft over a relatively short period forced his company to the brink of bankruptcy. The amount of his total loss was difficult to assess, but the figure was certainly approaching $500,000.

Willis took another sip of his martini and remembered the days when his business was thriving. Before three spreads of heavy earth-moving equipment had been stolen, the business was averaging a gross of over $300,000 a month. With the machinery gone, sales dropped to a pittance, cutting off his cash flow. His problems compounded. He was faced with the task of having to lay off 150 employees. It had all started with the loss of that expensive heavy equipment. If there were only some way he could get it back without dishing out more funds. . . .

Willis was greeted by Mark Evans, a successful general contractor. Willis liked Mark. He was always in good spirits, had a great sense of humor, and had the knack of making others feel good when he was around. Maybe that was why he was president of the Allied Contractors Association.

After a little small talk, Willis could no longer disguise his true feelings and simply broke down and told Evans of the problems his business was experiencing. Evans listened attentively, just as he would for anything else. At fifty below zero, Evans would shed his own coat to stop a friend from freezing. That's the kind of guy Evans was, Willis knew. "Have you met Dolan?" Evans asked after Willis finished his story. Willis had not. Evans then called over a fellow who was standing a short distance from them. Willis had seen the man at most of the contractors' functions. He seemed to get along well with everybody—everyone seemed to like him. Willis had assumed he was just another contractor.

As Dolan approached them, Willis could not help thinking that Dolan seemed every bit as self-assured and content as he himself had looked not long ago. Dolan *looked like a businessman*. After brief introductions, Evans informed the two men that he had to leave but mentioned to Willis that Dolan might be able to help him with some of his problems.

Willis then recounted his troubles to Dolan, who turned out to be a construction equipment salesman. Dolan told Willis that he often sold heavy equipment at discount prices to his friends and that anyone who was a friend of Evans was a friend of his. Willis was amazed when Dolan told him that he might have three spreads of heavy earth-moving equipment in stock and was doubly shocked when Dolan quoted him the price. The "discount" was nearly 75 per cent off the normal price. Willis couldn't believe it. How could he afford to sell so low?

"Because I'm a hell of a nice guy," Dolan laughed as he slapped Willis on the shoulder. "I've got to run now. I'll give you a call on that equipment."

That afternoon Willis got a call from Dolan who said that he not only had the equipment in stock but could deliver it the next afternoon. Was he interested? Willis was tempted to say "yes" before Dolan changed his mind. However, he was skeptical about the condition of the equipment since the quoted price was so low. So he agreed to a tentative purchase on the condition that the equipment was of at least fair quality.

The equipment turned out to be almost new and Willis was again dumbfounded. He signed the invoice accepting the order, noting the name at the top of the bill: "Pacific Construction Equipment, P.O. Box 464, San Francisco, CA 94609." He had never heard of the company before but he would be sure to keep a copy of the invoice for his records. That way, if anyone ever came around asking any questions, he'd have proof. . . .

During the next few months Dolan turned out to be the answer to Willis' prayers. Willis had the opportunity to buy equipment from Dolan a number of times after their initial deal. Business was booming again and Willis was making bigger profits than ever before. Thanks to Dolan he was making big savings on equipment purchases, savings that were invested and were producing more income for him and his family. Also, it seemed that equipment thefts from his job site were occurring less and less often. He got to know a lot of other contractors who were also dealing with Dolan. His position among the contractors seemed to take a dramatic turn for the better. Before, he always seemed to be on the outside looking in; now, at last, he felt like "one of the guys."

Sometimes he wondered where Dolan got the equipment and how he could sell it so cheaply. But it was not difficult to dismiss his suspicions. The other day, for example, his foreman pointed out that a few pieces of the equipment just purchased from "Pacific" had the serial numbers scratched out. Who was he to question Dolan's integrity? A good many other contractors with businesses more established and more financially capable than his own were also buying from Dolan. If they didn't see anything wrong with the operation, why should he?

Dolan sat at his desk and read aloud the last item on the Security Bulletin that had been circulated to the contractors as a part of Jobsite Security Week: "And remember, if a suspicious-looking character comes into your office one day with a super bargain, get his license plate number, remember as much about his physical characteristics as possible, and then call the police." Only an amateur salesman would operate like that, he thought. He chuckled a little when he came to the part about "call the police." The Security Bulletin originated in a county where at least ten police officers were on his "labor force."

Dolan had started out as a construction worker and a warehouse salesman, experience that gave him a good background for excelling in his present line of work. As a construction worker, he discovered early the value of construction tools and equipment. After work and under the cover of darkness, young Dolan would return and load his pickup with power tools left at the job site. He would then sell this equipment to other contractors in the area. Eventually he was caught and served a short term in prison, where he met and became friendly with many professional burglars, some of whom specialized in construction site theft.

Upon release from prison Dolan got a job as a warehouse construction supply clerk, having managed to keep his past a secret. In this job he learned a lot more than the fundamentals of supply requisitioning and documentation. He noticed that the origin of much of the equipment that came in for inventory was questionable.

Occasionally, two husky men would drive up to the warehouse with a truckload of goods. They would speak briefly with the boss, usually behind closed doors and in low voices. The equipment was then unloaded and added to the inventory stock. Dolan noticed that serial numbers had been obliterated and that some of the larger equipment smelled of fresh paint. It didn't take a genius to know that something wasn't "kosher." The purchasing contractors didn't seem to mind, however; they appeared more concerned with the amount of the "discount" than with the origin of the equipment.

Soon Dolan felt he had learned enough to go into business for himself. From the professional burglars he knew from prison and others he had met through his warehouse job, he selected five to do the actual ripoff work. Dolan would then go out to meet contractors at their regular meetings and informal gatherings at cocktail lounges and parties. Eventually, he got to know the contractors and their needs. Usually a contractor would subtly let it be known that he was in need of equipment of a certain type. Dolan would then inform him, initially in person but after that almost always by phone, that he expected such an item to be "turned in" within a few days. He would make the deal and then notify his "labor force" that the item was needed. The burglars were efficient, smooth, professional. No piece of equipment was impossible for them to steal. Big-wheel compressors, tractors, bulldozers—no problem.

Much of what was stolen in the Bay Area was resold in the Los Angeles region or in nearby states; and much of what was stolen from the Los Angeles region was resold to Bay Area contractors. Dolan's job required frequent travel back and forth between the different areas. He knew the contractors in Los Angeles as well as he knew those in the Bay Area.

Dolan's hired help were well equipped. The heists were made with rented trucks and other rented transport. After the theft the truckload of goods was transported to its destination and kept in an abandoned barn or some other convenient hiding place where necessary alterations were made before delivery.

Dolan had taken the extra precaution of having invoices printed under the names of ten fictitious construction equipment companies. Thus, when delivery was made (usually C.O.D.), it had all the trappings of legitimacy. The contractors liked it better that way. Although they never asked questions, Dolan knew that they did not for one minute consider that the operation was a legal one; he also knew that, as long as their pockets were full, they did not care where the equipment came from—as long as it did not come from their own job site.

Whenever possible, Dolan did not steal from a contractor who was his customer. A demonstration of good will and fair play, one might call it. Dolan realized that if he were arrested tomorrow, someone else would take his place within hours, mainly because the contractors wanted to do "business as usual." "Yes," Dolan thought, "it sure is funny. I earn my living by ripping off contractors, and yet contractors are my best customers. They keep me in business. But they think I keep them in business, too, so as long as they keep asking for it, I'm going to keep giving it to them."

Construction Site Theft as Organized Crime

The narrative presented above is the story not of one experience but of many. Only the names and a few details are fictional. The salesman is not always a freelancer like Dolan—sometimes he is a fence; sometimes a warehouse salesman. In New Jersey, where an operation similar to the one described above was detected and dismantled, the salesman was an established and reputable contractor.

The hired help does not always consist of ex-convicts.

Sometimes they are employed construction workers; in other cases they are people in positions of authority. Recall when Dolan "chuckled a little when he came to the part about 'call the police.' The Security Bulletin originated in a county where at least ten police officers were on his 'labor force.'" This assertion is not fictional, not far-fetched. On September 4, 1974, a front-page story of the *Oakland Tribune* opened with the following: "Four more Contra Costa County sheriff's deputies have resigned in the face of an investigation of burglaries at construction sites in the county. . . . Seven deputies have now quit the department as a result of the probe." Although the subsequent investigation led to a large turnover in personnel in the department, no attempt was made to determine the organizational structure of these burglaries.

From what we have seen, construction site crime can involve the institutions of racketeering (fencing), government (law enforcement agencies), business (warehouse salesmen and contractors), and labor (when burglars are construction workers). It could include the political arena if it is considered that no official pushed for a more thorough investigation of the Contra Costa incident.

According to . . . [a] new and more extensive definition . . . "organized crime" involves a group of at least ten persons who conspire to commit crimes for at least a year, guaranteeing each a substantial amount of money. The conspiracy must involve two or more of the institutions of racketeering, business, politics, labor, and government. The relationship between these institutions must be symbiotic.

Construction site crime meets all of the foregoing requisites. . . .

Conclusion

The stealing of heavy equipment from construction sites is an organized, systematic, criminal conspiracy designed to fatten the wallets of burglars, illicit salesmen, and legitimate businessmen. This system is encouraged and sustained by contractors within the construction industry, many of whom obviously cannot resist a bargain when it is offered. Once the initial deal is consummated, future purchases at bargain rates become irresistible to the contractor as he grows accustomed to a higher level of profit.

One reason for this situation is the capitalist business ethic: business is set up to make money and there is no effective limit on the individual accumulation of wealth. The only catch is that, under competitive conditions, supposedly only the strong survive. Organized crime in the construction industry protects against competition and gives the contractor a feeling of security in an insecure situation.

Is there a solution to the problem of organized crime in the construction industry? The few sincere attempts made so far to stop it have not been aimed at dismantling the organizational structure of the operation. Law enforcement efforts usually focus on amateur and nonprofessional thieves. . . .

Preventive programs initiated by contractors themselves, emphasizing the identification of equipment or the use of burglar alarms, locks, guard dogs, etc., are of even less value.

Most construction-site crime prevention programs appear to be designed only to appease the honest contractor by making him feel that something is being done or that there is something he can do. A few of the most visible and most vulnerable individuals are caught (usually the poor, the young, and the minorities) and everyone believes that the program is working and the crime rate is on the way down. Actually, petty criminals, whose thefts constitute a small fraction of the profits enjoyed by organized crime, are arrested while the larger criminal structure is allowed to persist.

During the study reported here, it often appeared that the contractors did not really want to dismantle the criminal organizational structure. Even the honest contractor fails to look beyond the individual burglar in such an operation, perhaps because he realizes that many of his friends are involved in such activities and he does not want to see them go to jail. For whatever reasons, the program examined for this report did not meet with initial success. The only real solution [to construction-site crime] depends on a factor beyond the control of the law: the honesty and morals of the individual contractor.

IV. THE MAKING OF A CRIMINAL

EDITOR'S INTRODUCTION

What induces some people to be criminals—if only for a few brutal moments? The next two sections consider this question from a number of points of view, following the research of one hundred years of criminology.

Talcott Parsons, the sociologist, described three major systems that he felt guided human actions. The three systems are personality, culture, and society. According to Parsons, the interplay of psychological forces within the individual make up the personality system, while values and norms provide the touchstones of the culture system. The social system however, has a structure all its own, built through the interaction of groups and individuals. By interacting, the three systems can encourage the actions of saints as well as criminals, many behavioral scientists believe.

In the first selection, Virginia Adams, an editor on the staff of the New York *Times,* surveys some of the major theories that have been raised to explain criminal behavior. Most of them fall into one or another of Parsons' systems; rarely do they straddle all three, because most scientists are specialists, expert in one area of knowledge, rarely two or three areas. Nonetheless, any satisfactory explanation of the causes of crime must account for the roles of all three systems of behavior.

Cesare Lombroso's nineteenth-century theory of the "born criminal" erred because it was too simple, as Stephen Jay Gould emphasizes in this section's second article, reprinted from *Natural History.* Gould, a professor of biology and the history of science at Harvard University, also points out the dangers of any attempt to place the blame for crime on genetic factors.

Patrick Young, a science and medical writer, explores another controversial explanation of criminality in this section's final piece, "A 'Criminal Personality'?" The explanation—painstakingly developed during years of research at a Washington, DC, mental hospital—puts the responsibility for crime on the criminal's personality.

THE CAUSES OF CRIME—MAYBE[1]

Cesare Lombroso was performing an autopsy on a bandit called Vilella when the "revelation" struck him.

The 19th-century Italian surgeon saw that the brigand's ears stuck out and that he had enormous jaws, high cheekbones, prominent bony arches above his eyes and a powerfully built body. In his book "The Criminal Man," Lombroso described his reaction: "I seemed to see all of a sudden, lighted up as a vast plain under a flaming sky, the problem of the nature of the criminal—an atavistic being who reproduces in his person the ferocious instincts of primitive humanity and the inferior animals."

If only it were that easy to understand crime. Lombroso is one of a long line of researchers to look for a simple explanation of criminal behavior. Scientists have never been able to agree on any one theory; today most of them recognize that the causes of crime are infinitely complex, and that none of the theories so far advanced can fully account for all crime. Yet some theories—generally those that are psychological or sociological rather than biological—do shed at least *some* light on *some* crimes.

Lombroso's hypothesis was of course biological, a badseed theory according to which criminals are born, not made. Inspired by Vilella and equipped with calipers and a tape measure, Lombroso examined a group of criminals and soldiers for receding chins, "excessively" long arms, unusually shaped heads and other "stigmata," as he called

[1] Article by Virginia Adams, editor, *The Week in Review. The New York Times*. Sec. IV, p 8. D. 18, '77. © 1977 by the New York Times Company. Reprinted by permission.

them. When he found more "anomalies" in the criminals
than in the soldiers, he thought he had proved that body
characteristics in some sense cause crime. Not surprisingly,
his theory did not stand up.

A more recent biological theory linked violent criminality with the so-called XYY defect in men. Normally, men's
cells have two chromosomes, a female X and a male Y;
XYY men are born with an extra Y. Some studies of imprisoned criminals have found numerous males with the
XYY pattern. But Dr. Fred Sergovich, a geneticist, observes
that "if you look only at abnormal populations, you will
find only abnormal XYY's." He estimates that the XYY
pattern occurs once in 1,000 or so male births and suggests
that if the general population could be surveyed, many law-
abiding XYY's would probably be discovered.

The latest XYY study, reported last year, was done in
Denmark by Dr. Herman Witkin, a senior research psychologist at the Educational Testing Service in Princeton,
N.J., and his colleagues. Screening a broad population,
they found a higher rate of convicted criminals among
XYY's than among chromosomally normal males. However,
the misdeeds of the convicted men were not notable for
their sophistication, and the researchers believe that the
elevated XYY rate they observed "may reflect a higher detection rate than a higher rate of commission."

In any event, the XYY men in the study were minor
offenders, and the investigators found "no evidence that
XYY men are more likely to commit crimes of violence
than men without the extra Y chromosome."

Psychologically minded theorists often think of crime
as a symptom of mental illness—or as an alternative to it.
The psychiatrist Seymour Halleck believes that a person
who feels utterly helpless to control his fate may unconsciously choose crime rather than mental collapse because
breaking the law can give a liberating sense of power.
"During the planning and execution of a criminal act,"
Dr. Halleck said, "the offender is a free man. He is immune

from the oppressive dictates of others since he has temporarily broken out of their control."

To Freud, "guilt was the real motor of crime." Committing a crime, he thought, can transform obscure feeling
of self-reproach into a guilt that is easier to bear because it
is at least comprehensible. Another psychoanalyst, Theodore
Reik, believed that a person may break the law because he
is driven by an unconscious need for punishment. "The
prospect of punishment," Reik said, "does not deter the
criminal but unconsciously drives him to the forbidden
deed."

Many psychiatrists think that some crimes are prompted
by the perpetrator's need to make his mark. ("I wanted
to be known," one murderer said to explain his deed.)
Even more often, it is argued, crimes are committed in
revenge for a loveless childhood. "The injustices perpetrated
upon a child," the psychoanalyst Karl Menninger wrote,
"arouse in him unendurable reactions of retaliation which
the child must repress and postpone but which will sooner
or later come out in some form or other." Many violent
criminals, psychiatrists have observed, were the objects of
violence when they were children.

In contrast to the psychological theorists, sociologists
look for causes outside the criminal rather than within
him. Edwin M. Schur of New York University cites "widespread corruption and hypocrisy that undermine respect
for law," as well as "degrading social conditions that en-
gender extreme alienation."

Statistically, the link between poverty and crime is un-
deniable; when joblessness rises, so does crime. But William
Vogel, Director of Psychological Research at Worcester
(Mass.) State Hospital, spoke for many experts when he
said that there is "no evidence of a one-to-one relationship
between poverty and crime." Most poor people are honest,
he noted, while many rich ones are not.

Since the early 1960's, many behavioral scientists have
been saying that some causes of some crimes may lie in

its victims. They may be provocative, or masochistic, or possess some personality trait—ambition, for instance—that "offends the offender," in the words of [the criminologist] Stephen Schafer. In this vein, the psychologist Richard Evans said after the murder of Robert Kennedy that the Kennedys were "victims in search of assassins."

In a now classic study of 588 Philadelphia murders, the criminologist Marvin E. Wolfgang concluded that 150 were "victim-precipitated homicides," that is, murders in which the eventual victim had been "the first in the homicide drama to use physical force." In a typical case described by Dr. Wolfgang, "A drunken husband, beating his wife in their kitchen, gave her a butcher knife and dared her to use it on him. She claimed that if he should strike her once more, she would use the knife, whereupon he slapped her in the face and she fatally stabbed him."

Interesting as their theories are, the victimologists have not really explained crime; no one has. "The fact is, those of us who study criminal behavior do not know the answer to the central question of why one person turns to crime when nine of ten persons raised in similar circumstances do not," Dr. Vogel said.

Yet every plausible sounding theory of causation has its advocates. Dr. Vogel believes the reason is simple: "It is more comforting to believe we have the answer to the why of criminal behavior than to accept the fact that we don't."

CRIMINAL MAN REVIVED[2]

W. S. Gilbert directed his potent satire at all forms of pretension as he saw them. For the most part we continue to applaud him: pompous peers and affected poets are still legitimate targets. But Gilbert was a comfortable Victorian at heart, and much that he labeled as pretentious now

[2] Article by Stephen Jay Gould, professor of biology and history of science, Harvard University. Reprinted with permission from *Natural History Magazine*. 85:16–18. Mr. '76. Copyright © the American Museum of Natural History, 1976.

strikes us as enlightened—higher education for women, in particular.

> A women's college! maddest folly going!
> What can girls learn within its walls worth knowing?

In *Princess Ida,* the Professor of Humanities at Castle Adamant provides a biological justification for her proposition that "man is nature's sole mistake." She tells the tale of an ape who loved a beautiful woman. To win her affection, he tried to dress and act like a gentleman, but all necessarily in vain, for

> Darwinian Man, though well-behaved,
> At best is only a monkey shaved!

Gilbert produced *Princess Ida* in 1884, eight years after an Italian physician, Cesare Lombroso, had initiated one of the most powerful social movements of his time with a similar claim made in all seriousness about a group of men —born criminals are essentially apes living in our midst. Later in life, Lombroso recalled his moment of revelation:

In 1870 I was carrying on for several months researches in the prisons and asylums of Pavia upon cadavers and living persons, in order to determine upon substantial differences between the insane and criminals, without succeeding very well. Suddenly, the morning of a gloomy day in December, I found in the skull of a brigand a very long series of atavistic anomalies. . . . The problem of the nature and of the origin of the criminal seemed to me resolved; the characters of primitive men and of inferior animals must be reproduced in our times.

Biological theories of criminality were not new, but Lombroso gave the argument a novel, evolutionary twist. Born criminals are not simply deranged or diseased; they are, literally, throwbacks to a previous evolutionary stage. The hereditary characters of our primitive and apish ancestors remain in our genetic repertoire. Some unfortunate men are born with an unusually large number of these ancestral characters. Their behavior may have been appropriate in savage societies of the past; today, we brand it as criminal. We may pity the born criminal, for he cannot help himself; but we cannot tolerate his actions. (Lombroso believed that about 40 percent of criminals fell into this category of innate biology—born criminals. Others committed misdeeds for greed, jealousy, extreme anger, and so on—criminals of occasion.)

I tell this tale for three reasons that combine to make it far more than an antiquarian exercise in a small corner of forgotten, late-nineteenth-century history.

1. A generalization about social history: It illustrates the enormous influence of evolutionary theory in fields far removed from its biological core. Even the most abstract scientists are not free agents. Major ideas have remarkably subtle and far-ranging extensions. The inhabitants of a nuclear world should know this perfectly well, but many scientists have yet to get the message.

2. A political point: Appeals to innate biology for the explanation of human behavior have often been advanced in the name of enlightenment. The proponents of biological determinisim argue that science can cut through a web of superstition and sentimentalism to instruct us about our true nature. But their claims have always had a different primary effect: they are used by the leaders of class-stratified societies to assert that a current social order must prevail because it is the law of nature. Of course, no view should be rejected because we dislike its implications. Truth, as we understand it, must be the primary criterion. But the claims of determinists have always turned out to be prejudiced rubbish, not ascertained fact—and Lombroso's criminal anthropology is the finest example I know. Biological determinism is a dangerous game for liberals (and a godsend for conservatives and apologists for the status quo).

3. A contemporary note: Lombroso's brand of criminal anthropology is dead, but its basic postulate lives on in popular notions of criminal genes or chromosomes. These modern incarnations are worth about as much as Lom-

broso's original version. Their hold on our attention only illustrates the unfortunate appeal of biological determinism in our continuing attempt to exonerate a society in which most of us flourish by blaming the victim.

This year [1976] marks the centenary of Lombroso's founding document—later enlarged into the famous *L'uomo delinquente (Criminal Man)*. Lombroso begins with a series of anecdotes to assert that the usual behavior of lower animals is criminal by our standards. Animals murder to suppress revolts; they eliminate sexual rivals; they kill from rage (an ant, made impatient by a recalcitrant aphid, killed and devoured it); they form criminal associations (three communal beavers shared a territory with a solitary individual; the trio visited their neighbor and were well treated; when the loner returned the visit, he was killed for his solicitude). Lombroso even brands the fly catching of insectivorous plants as an "equivalent of crime" (although I fail to see how it differs from any other form of eating).

In the next section, Lombroso examines the anatomy of criminals and finds the physical signs (stigmata) of their primitive status as throwbacks to our evolutionary past. Since he has already defined the normal behavior of animals as criminal, the actions of these living primitives derives from their nature. The apish features of born criminals include relatively long arms, prehensile feet with mobile big toes, low and narrow forehead, large ears, thick skull, large and prognathous jaw, copious hair on the male chest, and diminished sensitivity to pain. But the throwbacks do not stop at the primate level. Large canine teeth and a flat palate recall a more distant mammalian past. Lombroso even compares the heightened facial asymmetry of born criminals with the normal condition of flatfishes (both eyes on one side of the head)!

But the stigmata are not only physical. The social behavior of the born criminal also allies him with apes and living human savages. Lombroso placed special emphasis on tattooing, a common practice among primitive tribes and European criminals. He produced voluminous statistics on the content of criminal tattoos and found them lewd, lawless, or exculpating (although he had to admit one read: *Vive la France et les pommes de terre frites*—"long live France and french fried potatoes"). In criminal slang, he found a language of its own, markedly similar to the speech of savage tribes in such features as onomatopoeia and personification of inanimate objects: "They speak differently because they feel differently; they speak like savages, because they are true savages in the midst of our brilliant European civilization."

Lombroso's theory was no work of abstract science. He founded and actively led an international school of "criminal anthropology" that spearheaded one of the most influential of late-nineteenth-century social movements. Lombroso's "positive," or "new," school campaigned vigorously for changes in law enforcement and penal practices. They regarded their improved criteria for the recognition of born criminals as a primary contribution to law enforcement. Lombroso even suggested a preventive criminology —society need not wait (and suffer) for the act itself, for physical and social stigmata define the potential criminal. He can be identified (in early childhood), watched, and whisked away at the first manifestation of his irrevocable nature (Lombroso, a liberal, favored exile rather than death). Enrico Ferri, Lombroso's closest colleague, recommended that "tattooing, anthropometry, physiognomy . . . reflex activity, vasomotor reactions [criminals, he argued, do not blush], and the range of sight" be used as criteria of judgment by magistrates.

Criminal anthropologists also campaigned for a basic reform in penal practice. An antiquated Christian ethic held that criminals should be sentenced for their deeds, but biology declares that they should be judged by their nature. Fit the punishment to the criminal, not to the crime. Criminals of occasion, lacking the stigmata and capable of reform, should be jailed for the term necessary to secure their amendment. But born criminals were condemned by their nature: "Theoretical ethics passes over

the diseased brain, as oil does over marble, without pene-
trating it." Lombroso recommended irrevocable detention
for life (in pleasant, but isolated surroundings) for any
recidivist with the telltale stigmata. Some of his colleagues
were less generous. An influential jurist wrote to Lombroso:

You have shown us fierce and lubricious orang-utans with
human faces. It is evident that as such they cannot act otherwise.
If they ravish, steal, and kill, it is by virtue of their own nature
and their past, but there is all the more reason for destroying them
when it has been proved that they will always remain orang-utans.

And Lombroso himself did not rule out the "final solution":

The fact that there exist such beings as born criminals, organi-
cally fitted for evil, atavistic reproductions, not simply of savage
men but even of the fiercest animals, far from making us more
compassionate towards them, as has been maintained, steels us
against all pity.

One other social impact of Lombroso's school should be
mentioned. If human savages, like born criminals, retained
apish traits, then primitive tribes—"lesser breeds without
the law"—could be regarded as essentially criminal. Thus,
criminal anthropology provided a powerful argument for
racism and imperialism at the height of European colonial
expansion. The same jurist who spoke so blithely of orang-
utans argued that modern European criminals would be
"the ornament and moral aristocracy of a tribe of Red
Indians." Lombroso, in noting a reduced sensitivity to pain
among criminals, wrote:

Their physical insensibility well recalls that of savage peoples
who can bear in rites of puberty, tortures that a white man could
never endure. All travelers know the indifference of Negroes and
American savages to pain: the former cut their hands and laugh
in order to avoid work; the latter, tied to the torture post, gaily
sing the praises of their tribe while they are slowly burnt. [You
can't beat a racist *a priori*. Think of how many Western heroes
died bravely in excruciating pain—Saint Joan burned, Saint Se-
bastian transfixed with arrows, other martyrs racked, drawn, and

quartered. But when an Indian fails to scream and beg for mercy, it can only mean that he doesn't feel the pain.]

If Lombroso and his colleagues had been a dedicated group of proto-Nazis, we could dismiss the whole phenomenon as a ploy of conscious demagogues. It would then convey no other message than a plea for vigilance against ideologues who misuse science. But the leaders of criminal anthropology were "enlightened" socialists and social democrats who viewed their theory as the spearhead for a rational, scientific society based on human realities. The genetic determination of criminal action, Lombroso argued, is simply the law of nature and of evolution:

We are governed by silent laws which never cease to operate and which rule society with more authority than the laws inscribed on our statute books. Crime appears to be a natural phenomenon . . . like birth or death.

In retrospect, Lombroso's scientific "reality" turned out to be his social prejudice imposed before the fact upon a supposedly objective study. His notions condemned thousands of innocent people to a prejudgment that often worked as a self-fulfilling prophecy. His attempt to understand human behavior by mapping an innate potential displayed in our anatomy served only to work against social reform by placing all blame upon a criminal's inheritance.

Of course, no one takes the claims of Lombroso seriously today. His statistics were faulty beyond belief; only a blind faith in inevitable conclusions could have led to his fudging and finagling. Besides, no one would look to long arms and jutting jaws today as signs of inferiority; modern determinists seek a more fundamental marker in genes and chromosomes.

Much has happened in the 100 years between Lombroso's formulation of his theory and our Bicentennial celebrations. No serious advocate of innate criminality recommends the irrevocable detention or murder of the unfortunately afflicted or even claims that a natural penchant for criminal behavior necessarily leads to criminal action. Still, the spirit of Lombroso is very much with us. When Richard Speck murdered eight nurses in Chicago, his defense argued that he couldn't help it because he bore an extra Y chromosome. (Normal females have two X chromosomes, normal males an X and a Y. A small percentage of males have an extra Y chromosome, XYY.) This revelation inspired a rash of speculation; articles on the "criminal chromosome" inundated our popular magazines. The naïvely determinist argument had little going for it beyond the following: Males tend to be more aggressive than females; this may be genetic. If genetic, it must reside on the Y chromosome; anyone possessing two Y chromosomes has a double dose of aggressiveness and might incline to violence and criminality. But the hastily collected information on XYY males in prisons seems hopelessly ambiguous, and even Speck himself turns out to be an XY male after all. Once again, biological determinism makes a splash, creates a wave of discussion and cocktail party chatter, and then dissipates for want of evidence. Why are we so intrigued by hypotheses about innate disposition? Why do we wish to fob off responsibility for our violence and sexism upon our genes? The hallmark of humanity is not only our mental capacity but also our mental flexibility. We have made our world and we can change it.

A 'CRIMINAL PERSONALITY'?[3]

Maurice knows the streets of Washington, from the gutter up. He can tell you about his 20-year narcotics habit that began during the Korean War, the credit-union fraud, the car thefts, the armed robberies, and how he escaped a prison term by copping an insanity plea. But he'd rather not. Maurice is working for the federal government now, reunited with his wife and two children, and proud

[3] Article by Patrick Young, freelance science and medical writer. Washington *Post*. p C5. N. 20, '77. Copyright © 1977, Field Enterprises, Inc., reproduced through the courtesy of Field Newspaper Syndicate.

of the home he owns and the garden he tends each summer. What Maurice will tell you is that he would be dead, jailed or dodging the police today, if it hadn't been for the late Dr. Samuel Yochelson and his controversial work at St. Elizabeths Hospital.

Yochelson, a psychiatrist, began work at St. Elizabeths in 1961, seeking to learn the difference between criminals who were mentally ill and those who weren't. After four years, he reluctantly concluded there was no difference. Rather, Yochelson decided, criminals are very much in control of themselves, and the criminal-insanity plea is a charade engaged in equally by the courts, the criminals and the psychiatrists.

But Yochelson didn't stop there. He continued his research, compiling long, detailed interviews with 255 male criminals—ranging in age from 15 to 55—and their relatives, girl friends, employers and acquaintances. By the time of his death in November, 1976, Yochelson had collected some quarter million pages of notes and evolved his own theory of criminal personality and treatment. That theory, outlined with psychologist Stanton E. Samenow in the first two volumes of "The Criminal Personality," a projected three-volume work, is now the subject of strong praise and harsh criticism.

Crime and violence top the list of American concerns. Yet in spite of millions of dollars spent and decades of research, no one knows for certain how to reduce crime or how to rehabilitate offenders. So not unexpectedly, the suggestion that criminals can be identified by their personality characteristics, and some reformed, has attracted some national attention.

Television and newspapers have reported on the St. Elizabeths research. Dr. Samenow, who joined Yochelson's research project in 1970, finds himself in demand as a speaker to crime-prevention groups and meetings of correction officials across the country. During a visit to Sacramento in September, he spent 45 minutes briefing California Gov. Jerry Brown, at Brown's request.

Criminal-justice authorities and prison psychologists have reacted favorably to "The Criminal Personality." But among research-oriented psychologists, the books are getting a very bad press. "In a word, the work was very sloppy," says Dr. Saleem A. Shah, a psychologist who heads the National Institute of Mental Health's Center for the Study of Crime and Delinquency.

Some research journals have dismissed the notion of a criminal personality with short, snide reviews. More thoughtful articles have raised questions about the study's basic design: the lack of any control group with which to compare findings, the lack of a standardized interview and the inadequate classification of the people studied by such things as age, education, socio-economic status and criminal behavior.

"Errors of Thinking"

Such criticism raises questions about the validity of the research effort, which cost just over $750,000. "There is a sense of disappointment that such resources were wasted," says Dr. James Breiling, a staff psychologist with NIMH's crime-and-delinquency center.

The Yochelson-Samenow thesis contends:

□ Criminals differ in personality from noncriminals, with criminals possessing 52 "errors of thinking" that set them apart. These thinking errors—shared by all criminals —relate to such things as fear, anger, pride, personal power, sentimentality, religion, sexuality, personal uniqueness, trust, pretentiousness, responsibility and lying. The anger of criminals is pervasive; they suffer no guilt from injuring others; they break promises without thought; they alternate between an exaggerated view of self-worth and an overpowering sense of worthlessness; they thirst for power; they crave excitement.

"None of these thinking patterns is unique to the criminal, but the criminal shows them in the extreme," Samenow says. Lying, for example, is a trait common to all humans. But the criminal lies incessantly, says Samenow:

"If he's going to the A&P, he'll say he's going to the Safeway."

□ The criminal's thinking errors emerge at an early age, as does criminal behavior. Some chronic offenders begin committing petty thefts as early as age 4; during his lifetime, each hard-core criminal commits "literally thousands of crimes" for which he is never arrested.

□ Career criminals are not mentally ill and they commit their crimes by free choice. Yochelson concluded from his work that such offenders, despite psychiatric diagnoses to the contrary, are sane and their crimes are the result of rational decisions. Some criminals do suffer bouts of mental illness, but when they do, they lose interest in committing crimes.

□ Hardened criminals can reform, if they choose to radically alter their thinking process, but most will not. Thirty men have completed 500 hours or more of treatment at St. Elizabeths in the program Yochelson devised, but Samenow regards only 10 of these as fully changed. Based on the St. Elizabeths experience, he estimates the number of criminals who would choose to reform at 10 to 20 per cent.

Samenow eschews the word "rehabilitation" and uses "habilitation" when describing the chronic offenders he works with. "When you think of how these people react, how their patterns go back to age 3 or 4, there isn't anything to rehabilitate," he says.

An Assault on the Ego

No one is drafted into Samenow's small counseling program; every man is a volunteer. The process begins with a series of long interviews, the first lasting three hours. During these interviews, the criminal is told he will get no sympathy; that he alone is responsible for his problems; that he and his crimes are contemptible; that sociological and psychological jargon won't be accepted as excuses for his behavior .

Then the criminal's life of crime and his inner thoughts

are described in general terms, using Yochelson's profile of the criminal mind. He is told he began committing crimes early, that he has committed many crimes, that he lies constantly, that he has periods when he contemplates suicide. It is a frontal assault on the ego.

Many criminals, Samenow says, are baffled and intrigued as they hear what sounds to them as their life history and inner thoughts laid before them by a stranger; some react with indignation. "I really did not see myself as a criminal," said a veteran con man now counted as one of the program's successes. "I told Yochelson he was a pompous ass."

Most decide against trying the program. Those who join find a life of rigorous discipline, flavored with a touch of Alcoholics Anonymous.

"We take the attitude that once a criminal, always a criminal," Samenow says.

Drinking, smoking and sex are forbidden for the first six months for unmarried men, and married men are allowed sex only with their wives. Program participants meet for a year in a group session, three hours a day, five days a week. They learn to analyze their thinking patterns, always alert to the 52 errors. They are required to keep a daily, detailed record, which they report and discuss at each day's meeting. Those who fail to conform are dropped and their parole or probation officers notified.

Samenow sees himself as a teacher, trying to teach criminals new thinking patterns. He tells the story of one man who referred to a girl he had seen but did not know as a "whore." The man was told his statement contained two thinking errors: making a judgment without facts, and having an exaggerated sense of his own uniqueness.

"Our program is important for two reasons," Samenow says. "First, because it is a profile of who the criminal is, and second, because it is a program for change. This is no panacea for the crime problem. But the cost of crime is enormous, so even if we can change only 20 per cent, it's worth the try."

Samenow would like to conduct a study among young

children—using the profile of thinking errors devised by Yochelson as a guideline—to identify the thinking and action patterns that result in criminal behavior. "Just as we try to identify learning disabilities and other problems when children are young, a similar attempt can be made in the area of crime," he says.

Samenow acknowledges this raises fundamental concerns that some children in such a study might be branded as criminals. "That fills me with horror," he says. "Really, what I'm talking about is another study of cognitive development. It seems to me that if society wants to do something about crime prevention, other than pay lip service, this kind of study is essential, provided careful attention is paid to civil liberties."

But one official of the National Institute of Mental Health predicts such a study will never be funded, primarily because the basis for the study—Yochelson's criminal-personality profile—is regarded as invalid by the people who review projects for approval.

"More an Art Than Science"

The notion of a criminal personality is an old, complex and controversial issue. There was a time, particularly in the 1930s and 1940s, when behavior was regarded as largely a function of personality. But this view faded as studies suggested that behavior was a factor also of the situation and the context in which an individual found himself. Thus today behavior is generally regarded by social scientists as a complex interaction.

Nonetheless the idea that criminals differ in personality in a recognizable way has struck a responsive chord among corrections experts. Dr. Eric Thompson, chief psychologist at the U.S. penitentiary at McNeil Island, Wash., calls the Yochelson-Samenow work "the best I've read on the kind of work I do." The *National Sheriff* wrote that the first volume "should be read by everyone seeking an insight into the criminal personality."

"In summary," wrote Robert B. Mills, chairman of

criminal justice programs at the University of Cincinnati in the journal *Criminal Justice and Behavior*, " 'The Criminal Personality' is a seminal work, rich in new concepts of criminal treatment, which will be closely studied by correctional counselors for years to come . . . it gives correctional counselors a blueprint to begin the serious work of criminal rehabilitation."

But research-oriented social scientists have leveled harsh criticisms, such as those of Dr. John Burchard, professor of psychology at the University of Vermont. . . .

"What they have done is more an art than science," Burchard says in an interview. "An impressive number of criminals were interviewed, but it was done very subjectively. There was no standardized interview. You're left to blind faith to interpret their data. I don't think you can build scientifically on the base of knowledge they've accumulated."

. . . Samenow defends the study and its conclusions. "Our approach is clinical," he says. "It is a valid method of gathering data, even though it does not meet the rigorous experimental-design criteria of many laboratory or academic social scientists. . . .

"I am not a missionary for any approach, especially our own. If our work is given a modest but long-term trial in the field, and if it doesn't add something effective to our coping with crime, discard it."

V. YOUTH, POVERTY, AND RACE

EDITOR'S INTRODUCTION

Shortly after World War I, criminologists began to look beyond personality for an explanation of criminal behavior. Personality, they began to see, existed in a social setting. People with a predisposition to commit criminal acts were more likely to commit them in certain social settings than in others. " 'Environment' is no longer regarded as a scene of action for the person," W. I. Thomas, a sociologist, wrote in 1920, "but as material out of which the personality itself is built."

People of a particular mental bent, then, learned crime —at home, on the block, in the neighborhood, at work— from people in their own group. They tried it, found it rewarding, and in some cases made it a career.

Criminologists began to explore the role of culture systems in encouraging criminality during the 1930s. Why does certain behavior—swearing, for example—seem normal in one social setting and abnormal in another? The answer seems to lie in culture—the norms, attitudes, and values held in common by members of a particular social group. Some youths are delinquents and others not, two criminologists wrote in the 1930s, because of "the differences in social values, norms, and attitudes to which the children are exposed. . . . Within the limits of his social world and in terms of its norms and expectations, the delinquent may be a highly organized and well-adjusted person." In fact, he may not even see himself as a criminal, a label, however, that is given him by people who share the values and norms of another, perhaps dominant, culture.

The interactions of culture with personality and society

are a common concern of the first five pieces that make up this section. The first selection, an article from *Time,* examines crimes among the young. People who are 17 or under make up about one fifth of the population of the United States, but they account for more than half of all serious crimes.

The proportion of people under 18 years of age is declining. In the second selection, Jackson Toby, director of the Institute for Criminological Research at Rutgers University, tells how this decline could be reflected in the nation's crime rates in the 1980s.

What is the environment like for children who must grow up in an urban slum? The third selection, "Slums and Slum Dwellers," is excerpted from a report by President Lyndon B. Johnson's Commission on Law Enforcement and Administration of Justice and provides a classic description of what it is like to grow up in the slums of an American city.

For 350 years, race and racism have shaped life in America. They are subjects impossible to ignore in any comprehensive discussion of crime. The authors of the next two selections, both blacks, are aware of this. They are aware, too, that blacks are disproportionately represented both as victims and as victimizers. Lee Brown, a criminologist who serves as the public safety commissioner of Atlanta, Georgia, defines the relationship of blacks and crime and traces the problem to "the socioeconomic conditions under which blacks live." John A. Davis, another criminologist, isolates the problem in the conflict between two cultures—one white, the other black. "Crime among blacks," he concludes, "is a complex *reaction* to oppression."

Is there a causal relationship between social deprivation and criminal behavior? Does poverty explain—even excuse —crime? In this section's final piece, Ernest van den Haag, a psychoanalyst, sociologist, and professor of social philosophy, gives a firm negative answer to these questions. In his words, "To have little or no money makes it tempting to steal . . . but a poor person is not shorn of his ability to control temptations."

THE YOUTH CRIME PLAGUE[1]

People have always accused kids of getting away with murder. Now that is all too literally true. Across the U.S., a pattern of crime has emerged that is both perplexing and appalling. Many youngsters appear to be robbing and raping, maiming and murdering as casually as they go to a movie or join a pickup baseball game. A new, remorseless, mutant juvenile seems to have been born, and there is no more terrifying figure in America today.

More than half of all serious crimes [murder, rape, aggravated assault, robbery, burglary, larceny, and motor vehicle theft] in the U.S. are committed by youths aged ten to 17. Since 1960, juvenile crime has risen twice as fast as that of adults. In San Francisco, kids of 17 and under are arrested for 57% of all felonies against people (homicide, assault, etc.) and 66% of all crimes against property. Last year in Chicago, one-third of all murders were committed by people aged 20 or younger, a 29% jump over 1975. In Detroit, youths commit so much crime that city officials were forced to impose a 10 P.M. curfew last year for anyone 16 or under.

Though offenders come from every ethnic group and environment, most are nonwhite kids whose resentments are honed and hardened in the slums. Usually they are victims themselves, abused or abandoned by parents who tend to have a history of crime, chronic alcoholism or emotional disturbances. About half of the violent juvenile crime is committed by black youths, and a large but indeterminate amount by Hispanics. Especially in ghettos of big cities, the violent youth is the king of the streets.

[1] From article in *Time*. 110:18–20+. Je. 11, '77. Reprinted by permission from *Time*, The Weekly Newsmagazine; Copyright Time Inc. 1977.

When he is caught, the courts usually spew him out again. If he is under a certain age, 16 to 18 depending on the state, he is almost always taken to juvenile court, where he is treated as if he were still the child he is supposed to be. Even if he has murdered somebody, he may be put away for only a few months. He is either sent home well before his term expires or he escapes, which, as the kids say, is "no big deal." Small wonder that hardened juveniles laugh, scratch, yawn, mug and even fall asleep while their crimes are revealed in court.

A New York teen-ager explained in a WCBS radio interview how he started at the age of twelve to rob old women. "I was young, and I knew I wasn't gonna get no big time. So, you know, what's to worry? If you're doin' wrong, do it while you're young, because you won't do that much time."

Another boy, 15, recalled why he shot a "dude": "Wasn't nothin'. I didn't think about it. If I had to kill him, I just had to kill him. That's the way I look at it, 'cause I was young. The most I could have got then is 18 months."

In Miami, Edward Robinson, 15, was accused of raping a housewife at knife point, even while police surrounded the home. "What you gonna do to me?" he sneered. "Send me to youth hall? I'll be out in a few hours." That taunt landed him in adult court. But his case was an exception. Most juvenile criminals are precluded from effective punishment. Says Andrew Vogt, executive director of Colorado's District Attorneys' Association: "In effect, we have created a privileged class in society."

That privileged class keeps enlisting ever younger members. Partly this is a response to juvenile laws. Older kids employ younger confederates—who tend to get off easily if caught—to push drugs, commit robberies and sometimes murder. In New Haven, two brothers, Ernest Washington, 16, and Erik, 14, along with four other kids, were arrested for robbing and killing a Yale student. Since Erik was underage, he confessed that he had pulled the trigger. He told New Haven Prosecutor Michael Whalen: "The most

you're going to give me is two years." Erik, in fact, was
bound over to adult court. At his trial last month, guess
what? Erik denied doing the shooting. It did not help. He
was convicted and sentenced to 15 years to life. Says
Whalen: "He showed no awareness of conscience or re-
morse. He grinned like crazy. He probably figures that
prison is not a hell of a lot worse than other places he's
been."

Aside from this sort of calculation, kids seem to be
developing a taste for sadism earlier in life. William S.
White, presiding judge of the Cook County, Ill., juvenile
court, thinks that a lower limit may have been reached:
"I don't expect a six-year-old to be committing homicides."
Don't be too sure. In Washington, D.C., a six-year-old boy
siphoned gasoline out of a car and poured it over a sleeping
neighbor. Then he struck a match and watched the man go
up in flames.

More girls are getting involved in violent crime. From
1970 to 1975, the arrest rate of girls under 18 for serious
offenses climbed 40%, v. 24% for boys. In 1975, 11% of all
juveniles arrested for violent crimes were female. Last
month Chicago police finally caught a gang of six girls,
aged 14 to 17, after they had terrorized elderly people for
months. Their latest crime: the brutal beating of a 68-year-
old man. "I was amazed," says Police Lieut. Lawrence
Forberg. "They were indignant toward their victims, and
none of them shed any tears. This is the first time I've
encountered young girls this tough."

The Killing Costs

Youthful criminals prey on the most defenseless victims.
The very young, the old, the lame, sick and blind are
slugged, slashed and shot. They have retreated with broken
limbs and emotional scars behind triple-locked doors. Many
never venture out at night; some do not even risk the streets
during the day. In confinement, their anguish is not heard.
Often poor and not well educated, they do not know where
to turn or how to complain.

So what's new? ponders the director of a juvenile facility in New York. The old folks have been assailed for years. The kids, he insists, have a "value system" of their own that should be respected. They are rebels, by his murky reckoning, against a society that does not give them a chance. One peculiar value is demonstrated by a teen-ager who prowls Manhattan's Upper East Side in search of eyes to gouge. To date, he has made known attempts on a bus driver, a journalist, an Egyptian tourist, the son of former Manhattan Democratic Party Leader Edward Costikyan and others. He was never locked up because he was underage.

Elizabeth Griffith, 84, a black woman, was beaten in her New York City apartment by two black teen-agers. "I didn't feel the blows because I was so numb from the choking," she recalled. "The big one hollered, 'Hit her!' and the little one would come over and hit me again. And I looked at the little one and said, 'Shame on you.' I saw death and I was dead, and I started to call the Lord. I was thinking to myself, 'What a nightmare, oh, what a nightmare!'" A nightmare shared by innumerable others who cannot count on the basic minimum of a supposedly civilized society: personal safety. Says Jim Wilson, a black homicide detective in Harlem: "Anybody should be able to go out on the streets any time he wants."

Analysts tirelessly—and correctly—say that unemployment, slum housing, inadequate schools and the pathology of the ghetto contribute to the spreading scourge of youth crime. But the reverse is also true: the ripple effects of crime eventually overwhelm a city and destroy its *élan*. People are frightened away from downtown, reducing business for stores, theaters, restaurants. In their place, thick as weeds, sprout porno houses, massage parlors and gambling havens, where criminals thrive.

Crime is decimating communities like Harlem. Says William Lundon, a homicide detective: "It's as if there were a cancer out there, with the doctor operating every day." To ward off robberies, Harlem merchants—almost all of them blacks—often stay open 24 hours a day. But the longer they are around, the more chance there is that they will be assaulted. One all-night grocer, a genial man in his 60s who was shot in the stomach by robbers, lives permanently in the Alamo. Thieves managed to break through solid steel sheets over his windows; 20 cases of beer were lugged out through the skylight. "I couldn't have whipped my people into doing that," says the grocer in disbelief. Increasingly, Harlem businessmen are giving up in despair, contributing to the steady spiral of decline. In Queens, N.Y., a dozen plants employing some 1,000 people threatened for a while to relocate unless action was taken against the youth gangs that continually robbed them. The kids were so sure of not being punished that they even announced to the executives when they would strike next.

Schools are blamed, often justly, for not equipping children with the most elementary skills. But the schools in many cities have turned into criminal dens where the distraught teacher spends most of the time trying to keep order. The FBI reports that last year some 70,000 teachers were assaulted in U.S. schools and the cost of vandalism reached $600 million. Every school day an estimated 200,000 New York City kids are truant. At least some are fleeing the danger in the classroom. At a state legislative hearing this month, Felix Davila, 16, testified that he stayed away from school because gangs terrorized teachers and shoved girls into bathrooms where they were sexually molested or forced to take drugs. Miguel Sanchez, 16, told the committee that a gang called the Savage Nomads runs his school. "All they do is rape people, mug people. I got out."

The Elusive Causes

It takes a diligent search through history to discover another society that has been as vulnerable to its youthful predators. During the early days of the Industrial Revolution in England, gangs of rapacious children roamed the streets, filling passers-by with dread. But the youngsters' crimes had a clear purpose: destitute, they would kill for food.

Obviously, a relationship still exists between poverty and crime. But the connection is rather tenuous. The great majority of poor kids do not commit crimes. The persistent offenders may come from a ghetto, but they often have more money than the people they rob. Some earn enough from selling drugs and mugging to buy all they want and then some. Explains a juvenile thief: "You know, they don't wanta be wearin' the same old sneakers every day. They wanta change like, you know, they wanta pair of black sneakers." After buying sneakers, gobs of junk food, flashy clothes, a car and, of course, guns, what else does a growing boy need? Nothing, maybe, except kicks. Mugging is like "playing a game," says a youth who attends a school for problem kids in Manhattan. "Kids do it for the fun of it."

One kid, 14, and another, 17, pistol-whipped a woman carrying two bags of groceries to her home in Miami. As she lapsed into a fatal coma on the sidewalk, they continued to kick her, then walked off leaving the groceries. In Washington, two teen-age boys went to the home of a 100-year-old minister and asked for some water. When he let them in, one kid tried to garrote him and then the other slit his throat; somehow he survived. During a robbery in the same city, in which three men were killed and one was seriously wounded, a 15-year-old armed with a machete flailed away, as prosecutors described it, in "wanton, aimless destruction."

How can such sadistic acts—expressions of what moral philosophers would call sheer evil—be explained satisfactorily by poverty and deprivation? What is it in our society that produces such mindless rage? Was the 19th century French criminologist Jean Lacassagne right when he observed that "societies have the criminals they deserve"? Or has the whole connection between crime and society been exaggerated?

Some of the usual explanations seem pretty limp. Yes, America is a materialistic society where everyone is encouraged to accumulate as much as possible. Francis Maloney, commissioner of the department of children and youth in New Haven, notes that "merchants are upset about shoplifting. Well, all the goods are there on the rack to be taken. If you're trying to entice me with the tourist trap, the kid who hasn't money is going to take advantage too. We contribute to the offenses that are committed."

Yes, television glorifies violence and, yes, America is "permissive." In Madison, Wis., Dane County Judge Archie Simonson released a rapist, 15, into the custody of his family. Madison, the judge explained, is a sexually permissive community where women wear see-through blouses. The kid was only reacting "normally," said the judge, though the 16-year-old victim was wearing an unprovocative sweater. But surely these and similar arguments, which go to any length to hold society and not the individual accountable, are glib and shallow.

More serious analysts point to the fact that, historically, rapid economic expansion and ethnically mixed populations have produced crime—hence the waves of violence in the U.S. in the middle and late 19th century. Another factor that historically has been accompanied by crime, points out sociologist Marvin Wolfgang, is individual freedom. Some experts today argue that juvenile crime is spreading because everyone is pushing what he considers his "rights" to the utmost limits. Standards are lowered and blurred; any behavior, however deviant, finds its instant defenders. The traditional and constraining institutions of family, church and school have lost much of their authority. Says LaMar Empey, a University of Southern California criminologist who specializes in youth: "The 1960s saw the dissipation of the traditional controls of society. There was much more freedom of activity in all spheres, and it was inevitable that there would be more crime. Also, the admission that we had a racist society gave some people an excuse to attack that society without guilt."

Most important is the breakdown in the family. "The old saws about the family are true," says Judge Seymour Gelber, who hears 1,000 delinquency cases a year in Dade County, Fla. "We look for quick solutions, but family stability is the long-term answer." Adds Detective Ellen

Carlyle: "The parents don't seem to care. They turn to the police and say, 'Here's my problem. Take care of it.' But they must start caring for their children in infancy."

Gelber notes that blacks commit 75% of the violent crime in Dade County, though they constitute only 15% of the population. But Cubans make up a third of the county's population and account for only 12% of the violent crime. The judge believes the strong Cuban family structure explains this difference. Adds Juan Clark, a sociologist at Miami-Dade Community College: "Like the Chinese, the Cubans have close-knit families with more supervision. There are more three-generation families, and, customarily, middle- and upper-middle-class women do not work." But the stress of exile, as well as modern influences, is beginning to weaken Cuban families; gangs are forming and committing crimes.

For eleven years, Ned O'Gorman, a poet, has run a nursery school in Harlem where no kid is considered too far gone to be accepted. But O'Gorman claims few permanent successes; early parental influence is hard to shake. "The rate of failure," he says, "the return to the cycle that has been their lot and their families' lot forever, is enormous." By the time some youngsters reach O'Gorman at age three or four, their lives have been blighted by what can only euphemistically be called child abuse. Not only is the child cuffed around, but because of neglect, he risks being burned up in his bed, drowning in the bathtub, falling out the window. "In his eyes," says O'Gorman, "is the fixed stare of the blasted spirit."

Charles King, the black director of the Phoenix School, which provides therapy and schooling for 30 problem kids on Manhattan's Upper West Side, thinks that inconsistency of family treatment is more damaging to children than unrelieved harshness. First the parent strikes the kid, then lavishes gifts on him. The bewildered child has no way of telling right from wrong. He remains largely illiterate because no one talks to him. "His language," says King, "is not made to communicate, to establish relationships. It's rejection and rejection, it's the hell with it. The child learns that the only way to be heard is to kick somebody in the teeth. With violence, he suddenly becomes a being."

FEWER YOUTHS, LESS CRIME AHEAD[2]

Why will the United States crime rate in 1984 almost certainly be lower than it is today? For several reasons, one of them demography.

More than half the arrests for violent crime (murder, forcible rape, robbery and aggravated assault) are of persons 14 to 24 years of age, mostly males; two-thirds of the arrests for major property crime (burglary, larceny, motor-vehicle theft) are in that age group.

Fortunately, from the point of crime control, there will be about three million fewer persons 14 to 24 in 1984 than in 1977 although the population as a whole will be about 15 million larger. This means that the *number* of crimes committed in 1984 will decrease unless the relationship between criminal behavior and age changes in the next seven years, which is unlikely. The crime *rate* will decrease even more because the crime rate consists of the *number* of crimes divided by the population at the time.

How can demographers be so sure that there will be three million fewer persons 14 to 24 in 1984 than there are now? By extrapolating from births recorded 14 to 24 years earlier. Those who will be 24 in 1984 were born in 1960, just as the post–World War II baby boom was starting to taper off. Those who will be 14 in 1984 were born in 1970 when the birth rate was falling rapidly.

It is true that nonwhite crime rates are considerably higher than crime rates for whites. And it is also true that the nonwhite birth rate is about 50 percent higher than the white birth rate; consequently, there will be a greater

[2] Article entitled "A Prospect of Less Crime in the 1980's" by Jackson Toby, sociologist, director of the Institute for Criminological Research at Rutgers—The State University. New York *Times*. p 27. O. 26, '77. © 1977 The New York Times Company. Reprinted by permission.

proportion of nonwhites 14 to 24 in 1984 than the approximately 12 percent nonwhites in the general population. But this does not affect the prediction of lower crime rates in 1984. Nonwhite birth rates declined to about the same extent as white birth rates starting in 1960. The proportion of 14-to-24-year-olds to total population will be about the same in the minority community in 1984 as it is today.

These demographic changes will occur even if American tendencies to commit crimes remain exactly the same as at present. But there are at least two reasons to believe that American society will be in a better position to control crime in 1984 than it is now.

The first reason is that the United States is catching up with problems that seemed to be getting out of control during the 1960's.

Take the drug epidemic. Drug use and addiction struck large cities with disorganizing impact a decade and a half ago. But drug abuse will not continue to spread during the 1970's because drug abuse, like the crime problem it contributes to, is concentrated in adolescence and young adulthood. The declining birth rate of the 1960's will limit drug abuse in the 1980's even without the additional police, probation and parole officers, and treatment personnel recruited to cope with it.

However, the efforts of control agents will probably do some good—individual drug abusers will be rehabilitated or imprisoned more efficiently in the years ahead than during the past decade. Similarly, educational failure, another contribution to crime, will decrease in the 1970's, partly because fewer children will have to be educated than in the 1960's and partly because more teachers and facilities have accumulated to do the job. In short, crime will decrease to the extent that it was a symptom of problems that were accumulating faster in the 1960's than people and resources could be found to deal with them.

The second reason crime will fall in the 1980's is that crime is less likely to be considered morally justified now than it used to be. During the Vietnam War, an era of youthful radicalism, civil disobedience by "trashing" and by defying the police (and "ripping off the Establishment" by shop-lifting) seemed almost chic.

Crime as political protest never constituted a large proportion of total crime, even in the 14-to-24-year-old age group, but the influence of politically oriented offenders on ordinary criminals, particularly in the prisons, was to encourage recidivism.

An Eldridge Cleaver, who insisted that he raped white women to protest against racism in America, or a Karleton Armstrong, who blew up a University of Wisconsin building as a protest against the Vietnam War, gave even apolitical burglars and armed robbers a claim to moral superiority.

The decreasing plausibility of ideological justifications for crime in the years ahead will lower crime rates by motivating run-of-the-mill offenders to drop criminal pursuits *earlier* and concentrate on more conventional activities (jobs, family life). The process of maturing out of crime went on in the 1960's also, but anything that speeds the process up so that it occurs earlier appreciably reduces crime.

George Orwell notwithstanding, 1984 may yet be a good year.

SLUMS AND SLUM DWELLERS[3]

The slums of virtually every American city harbor, in alarming amounts, not only physical deprivation and spiritual despair but also doubt and downright cynicism about the relevance of the outside world's institutions and the sincerity of efforts to close the gap. Far from ignoring or rejecting the goals and values espoused by more fortunate segments of society, the slum dweller wants the same ma-

[3] From *The Challenge of Crime in a Free Society*. United States. President's Commission on Law Enforcement and Administration of Justice. Government Printing Office. Washington, D.C. '67. Text from Avon Books ed. '68. p 179–84.

terial and intangible things for himself and his children as those more privileged. Indeed, the very similarity of his wishes sharpens the poignancy and frustration of felt discrepancies in opportunity for fulfillment.

The slum dweller may not respect a law that he believes draws differences between his rights and another's, or a police force that applies laws so as to draw such differences; he does recognize the law's duty to deal with lawbreakers, and he respects the policeman who does so with businesslike skill and impartiality. Living as he does in a neighborhood likely to be among the city's highest in rates of crime, he worries about and wants police protection even more than people living in the same city's safer regions. He may not have much formal education himself, or many books in his house, and he may hesitate to visit teachers or attend school functions, but studies show that he too, like his college-graduate counterpart, is vitally interested in his children's education.

And while some inner-city residents, like some people everywhere, may not be eager to change their unemployed status, it is also true that many more of them toil day after day at the dullest and most backbreaking of society's tasks, traveling long distances for menial jobs without hope of advancement. Very likely his parents (or he himself) left home—the deep South, or Appalachia, or Mexico, or Puerto Rico—looking for a better life, only to be absorbed into the yet more binding dependency and isolation of the inner city. . . .

A sketch drawn from the limited information available shows that disproportionately the delinquent is a child of the slums, from a neighborhood that is low on the socioeconomic scale of the community and harsh in many ways for those who live there. He is 15 or 16 years old (younger than his counterpart of a few years ago), one of numerous children—perhaps representing several different fathers—who live with their mother in a home that the sociologists call female-centered. It may be broken; it may never have had a resident father; it may have a nominal male head who is often drunk or in jail or in and out of the house (welfare regulations prohibiting payment where there is a "man in the house" may militate against his continuous presence). He may never have known a grownup man well enough to identify with or imagine emulating him.

From the adults and older children in charge of him he has had leniency, sternness, affection, perhaps indifference, in erratic and unpredictable succession. All his life he has had considerable independence, and by now his mother has little control over his comings and goings, little way of knowing what he is up to until a policeman brings him home or a summons from court comes in the mail.

He may well have dropped out of school. He is probably unemployed, and had little to offer an employer. The offenses he and his friends commit are much more frequently thefts than crimes of personal violence, and they rarely commit them alone. Indeed, they rarely do anything alone, preferring to congregate and operate in a group, staking out their own "turf"—a special street corner or candy store or poolroom—and adopting their own flamboyant title and distinctive hair style or way of dressing or talking or walking, to signal their membership in the group and show that they are "tough" and not to be meddled with. Their clear belligerence toward authority does indeed earn them the fearful deference of both adult and child, as well as the watchful suspicion of the neighborhood policeman.

Although the common conception of the gang member is of a teenager, in fact the lower class juvenile begins his gang career much earlier, and usually in search not of co-conspirators in crime but of companionship. But it is all too easy for them to drift into minor and then major violations of the law.

That is not to suggest that his mother has not tried to guide him, or his father if he has one or an uncle or older brother. But their influence is diluted and undermined by the endless task of making ends meet in the face of debilitating poverty; by the constant presence of temptation—

drugs, drinking, gambling, petty thievery, prostitution; by the visible contrast of relative affluence on the other side of town.

The Physical Environment

It is in the inner city that the most overcrowding, the most substandard housing, the lowest rentals are found. Farther out in the city, more families own their own homes; presumably more families are intact and stable enough to live in those homes and more fathers are employed and able to buy them. The inevitable influence of slum living conditions on juvenile behavior need not be translated into sociological measurements to be obvious to the assaulted senses of the most casual visitor to the slum. Nor does the child who lives there fail to recognize—and reject—the squalor of his surroundings:

Well, the neighborhood is pretty bad, you know. Trash around the street, stuff like that and the movies got trash all in the bathroom, dirty all over the floors. Places you go in for recreation they aren't clean like they should be, and some of the children that go to school wear clothes that aren't clean as they should be. Some of them, you know, don't take baths as often as they should. Well, my opinion is . . . it's not clean as it should be and if I had a chance, if my mother would move, I would rather move to a better neighborhood. [16-year-old boy.]

It's sort of small. . . . It's something like a slum. Slum is a place where people hang out and jest messy, streets are messy, alleys are messes and a lot of dirty children hang around there. I would say it is a filthy place. [12-year-old boy.]

What the inner-city child calls home is often a set of rooms shared by a shifting group of relatives and acquaintances—furniture shabby and sparse, many children in one bed, plumbing failing, plaster falling, roaches in the corners and sometimes rats, hallways dark or dimly lighted, stairways littered, air dank and foul. Inadequate, unsanitary facilities complicate keeping clean. Disrepair discourages neatness.

Insufficient heating, multiple use of bathrooms and kitchens, crowded sleeping arrangements spread and multiply respiratory infections and communicable diseases. Rickety, shadowy stairways and bad electrical connections take their accidental toll. Rat bites are not infrequent and sometimes, especially for infants, fatal. Care of one's own and respect for others' possessions can hardly be inculcated in such surroundings.

More important, home has little holding power for the child—it is not physically pleasant or attractive; it is not a place to bring his friends; it is not even very much the reassuring gathering place of his own family. The loss of parental control and diminishing adult supervision that occur so early in the slum child's life must thus be laid at least partly at the door of his home.

The physical environment of the neighborhood is no better. In the alley are broken bottles and snoring winos—homeless, broken men, drunk every day on cheap wine. ("There are a whole lot of winos who hang around back in the alley there. Men who drink and lay around there dirty, smell bad. Cook stuff maybe. Chase you. . . ." [13-year-old.]) Yards, if there are any, are littered and dirty (". . . and the yard ain't right. Bottles broke in the yard, plaster, bricks, baby carriages all broken up, whole lot of stuff in people's yards." [14-year-old describing his home.]) The buildings are massive sooty tenements or sagging row houses. ("I don't like the way those houses built. They curve . . . I don't like the way they look. . . . They make the street look bad." [13-year-old.])

On some stoops, apparently able-bodied men sit passing away the time. On others children scamper around a grandmother's knees; they have been on the streets since early morning, will still be there at dusk. The nearest playground may be blocks away across busy streets, a dusty grassless plot. ("There ain't no recreation around. There was a big recreation right across the street and they tore it down. . . . [T]hey just closed it up—instead of building a road they put up a parking lot. . . . There ain't enough playgrounds, and if you go down to the railroad station, there is a big yard down there, . . . cops come and chase us off. . . ." [14-year-old boy.]) Harlem, for example, although it borders on and contains several major parks,

is generally lacking in play space. . . . [A]bout 10 percent of the area consists of parks and playgrounds, compared to over 16 percent for New York City as a whole. The total acreage of 14 parks and playgrounds is not only inadequate, but all the parks are esthetically and functionally inadequate as well. . . . For many of the children, then, the streets become play areas, and this, coupled with the heavy flow of traffic through the community, results in a substantially higher rate of deaths due to motor vehicles among persons under 25 (6.9 per 100,000 compared to 4.2 per 100,000 for all of New York City). [*Youth in the Ghetto* (Harlem Youth Opportunities Unlimited, Inc., 1964), pp. 100–101.]

In addition to actual dangerousness, lack of recreation facilities has been shown to be linked to negative attitudes toward the neighborhood and those attitudes in turn to repeated acts of delinquency.

Overcrowding alone is an obstacle to decent life in the slum. In central Harlem, the population density is approximately 66,000 people for every square mile—a rate at which all the people in the nation's 12 largest cities would fit inside the city limits of New York.

Even apart from its effects on the soul, such packing has obvious implications for the crime rate. Some crime is a kind of collision; when so many people are living and moving in so small a space, the probability of collisions can only increase. Crowding has a harmful effect on study habits, attitudes toward sex, parents' ability to meet needs of individual children; clearly, crowding intensifies the fatigue and irritability that contribute to erratic or irrational discipline.

Many of the people and activities that bring slum streets and buildings to life are unsavory at best. Violence is commonplace:

When I first started living around here it was really bad, but I have gotten used to it now. Been here 2 years. People getting shot and stuff. Lots of people getting hurt. People getting beat up. . . . Gee, there's a lot of violence around here. You see it all the time. . . . [14-year-old boy.]

Fighting and drunkenness are everyday matters:

Sometime where I live at people be hitting each other, fighting next door. Then when they stop fighting then you can get some sleep. . . . [15-year-old boy.]

Drinking, cussing, stabbing people, having policemen running all around mostly every day in the summertime. [14-year-old.]

Drug addiction and prostitution are familiar. The occupying-army aspects of predominantly white store ownership and police patrol in predominantly Negro neighborhoods have been many times remarked; the actual extent of the alienation thereby enforced and symbolized is only now being generally conceded.

BLACK VICTIMS, BLACK VICTIMIZERS[4]

The plight of blacks in respect to crime and criminal justice can clearly be seen in their disproportionate representation in arrest rates, victimization surveys, and jail and prison data. In examining crime for 1976, as reported by the FBI, we find that of those arrested for violent crimes, 47.5 percent were black. In the case of property crimes, 30.9 percent of those arrested were black. In respect to the cities, blacks accounted for 52.9 percent of all arrests for violent crimes, and 33.7 percent of all property crimes.

It is also important to note that in 1976, over 73 percent of those arrested for auto theft, murder, aggravated assault, robbery, and burglary were under the age of twenty-five; 59.6 percent were under twenty-one; 41.5 percent were

[4] Reprinted from "The Victimizers," article by Lee Brown, criminologist, public safety commissioner of Atlanta, Georgia. *The Nation's Cities.* 16:16–18. S. '78. Copyright © 1978 by the National League of Cities. Reprinted by permission.

under eighteen; and 16.1 percent of them were under fifteen.

A 1973 victimization survey conducted for the Law Enforcement Assistance Administration (LEAA) by the Bureau of Census revealed that black males were more likely than white males to have been victims of personal crimes. The survey showed that black males had a victimization rate of eighty-five per 1,000 as compared with that of seventy-five per 1,000 for white males. Furthermore, the same survey showed that blacks were more likely than whites to have been the victims of rape, robbery, and assault. Similarly, black males were more likely than white males to have been victims of aggravated assault. In respect to property crimes, black households had a higher burglary rate than white households in all income groups. In respect to larceny, the same was true. Also, blacks with incomes over $10,000 had a higher rate of victimization for motor vehicle theft.

An extremely important point that emerges from victimization survey data is that the poorer people are, the more likely they will become crime victims.

A review of who is in our jails and prisons further highlights the plight of blacks in respect to crime. In 1972, a jail survey conducted by LEAA revealed that 42 percent of all jail inmates were black, out of 141,600 persons in jail, 58,900 were black. It is also interesting to note that of the blacks confined in jails throughout the nation, almost 70 percent had not completed high school, 46 percent had been earning less than $2,000 a year when arrested, and another 12 percent had been earning less than $3,000 a year.

An examination of the composition of state prisons reveals a pattern similar to that of jails. An inmate census of state prisons conducted in 1973 for LEAA showed that about 48 percent of all prisoners were black. Of that number, at least 64 percent had not completed high school. In respect to age, 52 percent were under twenty-five, and 75 percent were under thirty.

At the federal level, the percentage of nonwhites confined in federal prisons has increased from 27.4 percent in 1969 to 38.2 percent in 1976.

The $420 Crime

To adequately depict the extent to which crime impacts upon black America, there is a need to know the economic, social, psychological, and political consequences of crime on black Americans.

If we examine the economic impact of crime, it is well to start with the total cost of crime in the United States. It has been estimated that crime costs approximately $420 per year for every person in the United States. Yet, just as crime impacts disproportionately on the black community, so does its cost.

Dr. Andrew F. Brimmer, while a member of the Board of Governors of the Federal Reserve System, estimated that in 1969, crime cost the black community about $3 billion of the $25 billion it cost the nation as a whole. In 1974, the cost of crime in the black community was still much higher. For example, it was estimated that blacks comprised about 12 percent of the nation's population in 1974, so using a very conservative estimation, blacks bore about 15 percent of the nation's cost of crime. It is estimated that crime cost the nation approximately $88.6 billion in 1974, thus, crime would have cost the black community approximately $13.29 billion in 1974. Considering the rate of inflation between 1974 and 1978, crime is even more costly to the black community today than in the past.

Brimmer also addressed the impact of crime on black businesses. He concluded that:

The situation of the average black businessman is equally distressing. Typically, he is a small-scale operator engaged in the provision of personal services or in low-margin retailing in the ghetto. For example, the president's commission estimated that losses in the retail field associated with crimes (such as shoplifting, employee theft, etc.) may amount to as much as 2 percent of the value of all retail sales. Since after-tax profit margins tend to be then in these lines (frequently in the range of 4 to 6 percent), this means that the crime toll may be eroding more than one-third of the net earnings of many black businessmen. Moreover, these figures do not include losses due to robbery which are known to inflict a staggering tariff on ghetto businessmen. With blacks taking over from whites more and more ghetto establishments, they are bearing an increasing share of the costs of crime. In fact, a significant proportion of failures—particularly among recently launched black businesses—can be traced to some extent to the adverse impact of crimes against them.

Whereas the economic impact is high, the social impact might be even greater. A national study conducted in 1972 revealed that 40 percent of the nonwhite respondents were afraid to walk alone at night. It is not unusual to see entire neighborhoods in black communities with bars on windows and doors resembling fortresses of old. Crime and the fear of crime have created a high level of social isolation which, in turn, limits social interaction and social solidarity that is necessary for the development of a sense of social well-being. It is quite likely that freedom from want may become all but meaningless if not accompanied by freedom from fear, and crime breeds fear.

Crime also has grave psychological consequences for the black community. The ever present possibility of being victimized, coupled with the unpredictable consequences of such victimization result in chronic anxiety, tension, and stress which are damaging to physical and mental health. Hence, such reactions of stress tend to produce increased aggressiveness, withdrawal (in different forms, including drug use), and the breakdown of interpersonal communications.

In addition, the disproportioned distribution of crime is used for political purposes as evidenced by "law and order" campaigns designed to obtain support and passage of repressive legislation that impacts negatively on the poor and blacks. It increases insurance rates; it changes socialization patterns, and it creates negative images in white communities about blacks as a group.

This assessment of the impact of crime on the black

community can best be summed up by saying that the poor, the powerless, the undereducated, and especially blacks are more likely to be arrested for criminal offenses, as well as become victims of criminal acts. Crime, be it white collar crime or street crime, has a disproportionate impact upon black Americans and represents a form of exploitation that must be addressed.

A Social Perspective

A brief review of the conclusions reached by researchers who have addressed the causes of crime in the black community provides a perspective upon which policy decisions can be based.

Mozell Hill, writing in the *Journal of Negro Education,* presented the perspective that blacks who live in blighted areas suffer deeply from discrimination, rejection, and lack of integration into the society. Juvenile delinquency among them is generated by this lack of integration, rather than by process of social disorganization. An increase in juvenile delinquency is likely to occur most frequently where aspirations of youths persist under conditions of limited and proscribed opportunities. Under such circumstances, access to success goals by legitimate means is seldom available to black youths in cities. They do not have opportunities for internalization of acceptable and respectable forms of conduct.

Morris Forslund conducted a study which compared black and white crime rates. He presents four factors to explain crime among blacks: the overrepresentation of blacks in the high crime risk, lower socioeconomic strata; the overrepresentation of blacks in high crime risk, younger age categories; the relative lack of opportunities for blacks to achieve their goals through legitimate means, and overrepresentation of blacks among the populations of the high crime, deteriorated sections of our cities which produces greater opportunities to learn criminal behavior patterns.

Ramsey Clark, former attorney general of the United States, in his discussion of the nature and causes of crime concluded that probably four in five of all serious crimes flow from places of extreme poverty, and most are inflicted on the people who live there. More specifically, he attributed crime to the problems of poor education, unemployment, bad health, and inadequate housing.

As can be seen from the preceding exploration of some of the causes of crime, crime in the black community is a result of the relative deprivation of black people.

The central theme that emerges on the subject of crime among blacks is the consistent reference to the plight of blacks in the socioeconomic arena. It can, therefore, be concluded that American social scientists, academicians, and practitioners who have examined this subject tend to agree that there is either a direct or indirect relationship between crime and the socioeconomic conditions under which blacks live. To control crime, therefore, there must be a commitment on the part of policy makers to solve those socioeconomic problems considered to be causative factors in criminal behavior.

BLACKS, CRIME, AND AMERICAN CULTURE[5]

Thirty-one years ago, Gunnar Myrdal stated that the Negro problem was not only America's greatest failure but also America's incomparable opportunity for greatness. He entitled his work *An American Dilemma,* and arguments raged as to whether or not a real dilemma existed in the minds and souls of white America. Since the mid-sixties, American blacks have argued that no dilemma exists, because white America has never accepted the black man as an equal human being.

The brutal suppression inflicted upon blacks by whites is the result of a paranoid state directly related to attitudes toward crime and blacks. The feeling is that crime is the embodiment of evil and blacks are therefore more "crime

[5] From article by John A. Davis, criminologist, University of California at Los Angeles. *Annals of the American Academy of Political and Social Science.* 423:89–98. Ja. '76. © 1976, by The American Academy of Political and Social Science.

prone" because they are more distant from "good," which is white. This dichotomous thinking is reflected in public attitudes as well as the formulations of criminologists about "causes" of crime.

Black Culture and the American Experience

The black man is seen as "made in America," his background and tradition buried in the watery graves of the millions who died on the passage over. He has no past worth mentioning, and his presence is seen as the expression of the tolerance of his benefactors. His future depends on his ability to internalize the dominant culture. However, there is a growing school of thought among black scholars that Afro-American culture has important differences from the dominant American culture. The foundation of this argument rests on the assumption that cultural habits are extremely resilient, so many of the African traditional modes remain, especially within the southern black population. Although the formal cultural structure (for example, family, communal living, social stability, and so forth) was destroyed by the institution of slavery, the habits remained, only severed from their roots. Blacks were left with habits and preferences which could not be understood and which were ridiculed by the dominant society. This cultural attack may have had consequences more detrimental to blacks than the personal attacks. The attempt to validate the inherent inferiority of blacks "scientifically" has been constant from the time of U. B. Phillips [in the early twentieth century] to the present arguments of Shockley and Jensen.

The systematic attack on blacks affected both blacks' and whites' attitudes, and the primary basis of the attack was cultural. Whites justified their racist practices through cultural attitudes and blacks suffered as a result. The suffering is expressed in various ways by social scientists, but the most direct expression is through the concept of self-hatred. This development was well understood by [the influential social philosopher Frantz] Fanon when he stated:

Every colonized people—in other words, every people in whose soul an inferiority complex has been created by the death and burial of its local culture originality—finds itself face to face with the language of the civilizing nation; that is, with the *culture* of the mother country. The colonized is elevated above his jungle status in proportion to his adoption of the mother country's cultural standards. (emphasis added)

The point to this is that, although the black man's culture may not have been destroyed, his understanding and appreciation of his culture was severely damaged. Afro-Americans were left in a cultural wasteland with no sense of belonging. Rejected and depreciated by the dominant American society, separated from and resentful of their African background, blacks were surrounded by a sea of cultural and personal confusion. They came to hate themselves. It is amazing that black people even survived the early American experience and a small wonder that blacks have tended to commit crimes against themselves.

Law and Inequality

One cannot understand crime without understanding the nature of the social order in which it occurs. Crime in America takes place within a capitalistic system where greater emphasis is placed on property rights than on human rights. The paramount value within the society is profit, and individual value is measured by the ability to amass profits. Those individuals having great wealth form a sort of Interest Group and influence the formation of laws to protect their interests. Only acts that violate laws are criminal, no matter how reprehensible the act. The great debate which followed Edwin Sutherland's work . . . [*White Collar Crime*] is an example of this definitional problem.

Statute law exists to protect the interests of powerful groups in the United States. These materialistic interests derived from profit are secured through exchange. Some men benefit and others are burdened by this exchange, and laws protect the system through which this unequal exchange is perpetuated. Therefore, in the area of property, the order which derives from the enforcement of laws perpetuates material inequality. Human value is attached to materialism, and those who own little or nothing have less value and, to the degree that they adopt the values of the system, lower self-esteem. This fact may be reflected in aggressive impulses resulting from despair, hopelessness, and frustration.

On the other hand, the laws regulating crime against persons may be more equal in the sense that they cover the interests of practically all groups in society and therefore reflect a lower level of inequality. However, the *dynamic* aspect of law (that is, enforcement) has been shown to reflect differences depending on the interest group of the victim and victimizer. There is also evidence to show that a definite relationship exists between economic exploitation and the potential to aggress against others. Edwin Schur reflects this position when he suggests that America is a criminal society because it is an unequal society. The oppression necessary to maintain an unequal system, and the inability to affect the imposing value system based on materialism, negatively affects the self-esteem of those burdened by the system.

Self-Esteem as Protest

Self-esteem, including self-respect and feelings of success, is based on a physical and social environment in which the person can find order and security. Much of the literature dealing with self-esteem assumes the importance of compatibility between the person and his environment. But what if a person is oppressed and is aware of the source and nature of his oppression? What if his or her burning desire is to remove the source of that oppression? Self-esteem then becomes functionally related to oppression. A particular form of opposition takes place: self-esteem is expressed in the form of protest, and protest takes on many forms.

Although there are many sources of oppression, the

dominant sources in America are economic and racial oppression. The action aspect of law is the mechanism used by the dominant society to keep opposition under control. Racial oppression has economic features. Indeed, the initial impetus to enslave blacks may have been primarily economic. However, the system developed to justify the perpetuation of slavery took on racial qualities independent of economic considerations. These developments had an impact on both blacks' and whites' beliefs and attitudes.

Although there is little hard data on early opposition to racial oppression among black slaves, we can gain some insight through the analysis of early folktales and folk heroes. "High John the Conqueror" is a folktale describing a folk hero who successfully resisted oppression through the use of his wits:

That's the kind of plantation John lives on. But it didn't bother John none. He was a *be* man. Wasn't no disputing that. High John loved living, and, although he was a slave, he made up in his mind that he was gon' do as much living and as little slaving as he could. He used to break the hoes—accidentally, of course. Set ol' mass'a barn of fire. Accidentally, of course. He always had a hard time getting to the field on time, and when he did get there, somehow the mule would accidentally tramp down a whole row of cotton before the boss man knew what was happening. Ol' massa was never sure, though, whether or not John was doing all this on purpose, because John would work real hard some years and make a good crop. The next year, though, it seemed like everything he touched got destroyed.

The theme of opposition to oppression is repeated over and over again in terms of either covert attacks on property owned by slaveholders or flight from the oppressive situation.

Opposition to oppression can also be seen in a number of accounts of slave resistances. The Denmark Vesey conspiracy of 1822 took place in Charleston, South Carolina. Slaves were enlisted from a distance of 80 miles, and thousands were involved. The 1831 publicized case of Nat Turner also involved thousands of rebellious slaves, and it was an up-

rising in which approximately 60 whites lost their lives
as did approximately 100 blacks. The response of whites
was to hang all participating and suspected blacks. Furthermore, night riders were organized to put down any secret
meetings among slaves. The night riders had the authority
of "policemen," and their expressed purpose was to intimi-
date and harass slaves.

Other blacks outside the South openly encouraged
slaves to rebel. Most notable of these calls was issued by
Henry Highland Garnet and David Walker. Garnet was a
twenty-seven-year-old Presbyterian minister who, in 1843,
stated:

Nearly three million of your fellow-citizens are prohibited by
law and public opinion (which in this country is stronger than
law) from reading the Book of Life. Your intellect has been destroyed as much as possible and every ray of light they have attempted to shut out of your minds. The oppressors themselves
have become involved in the ruin. They have become weak, sen-
sual and rapacious—they have cursed you—they have cursed themselves—they have cursed the earth which they have trod. . . . They
endeavor to make you as much like brutes as possible. When they
have blinded the eyes of your mind—when they have embittered
the sweet waters of life—then and not till then, has American
slavery done its perfect work. TO SUCH DEGRADATION IT
IS SINFUL IN THE EXTREME FOR YOU TO MAKE VOL-
UNTARY SUBMISSION.

David Walker was less eloquent and more direct. He
was an agent for a black newspaper in Boston, and he issued
an appeal to slaves which urged a bloody rebellion if the
oppressors did not grant liberty. According to William
Katz, the copies of his appeal were found throughout the
South and the slaveholders panicked, offering a reward for
Walker dead or alive. The occurrence of opposition to the
symbol of oppression (property) was much more frequent
than to persons, yet the few violent attacks on whites
kindled a deep fear in their hearts, and they reacted with
intense brutality. This set the stage for the public attitude
that the "criminal" acts against oppression were basically
against persons.

The legal decisions of the Supreme Court and the legislature generally reflected the public opinion, which was anti-slave. However, the fact that the North may have been anti-slavery does not mean it was pro-slave. Opposition to slavery was basically an economic phenomenon supported by powerful manufacturing interests. These interests were pitted against the equally powerful agrarian interest of the South, and the political compromise was a sort of balance-of-power decision reflected in a number of legislative decisions, such as the Missouri Compromise. The judiciary also reflected the guiding sentiment of that time. This culminated in the Dred Scott Decision of 1857, in which Judge Roger Taney declared that the Missouri Compromise was unconstitutional, stating that "the Negro has no rights which a white man is bound to respect." In the case of *Plessey* v. *Ferguson* (1898), the Supreme Court held that laws which segregate people because of their race did not violate the United States Constitution. This decision solidified the Separate but Equal Doctrine, which held until the Brown Decision in 1954. Even though the ruling had clear implications for desegregation of schools, we find that schools are as segregated today as they were then.

Clearly, blacks in this country could not redress their grievances through the law. The law and its enforcement was against the interests and well-being of the black man. Under such oppressive conditions, resistance to law is resistance to oppression. W. E. B. Dubois explored this problem in an early work. He described the Convict Lease System which developed in southern states after the Civil War. This system was a form of cheap labor for plantation owners who could "lease" blacks convicted of crimes. Since there were few jobs for blacks, a large number could easily be arrested as vagabonds. The system produced a large pool of laborers for agrarian interests.

The effect of the system on the black perspective was to link crime and slavery to white suppression. Dubois states that, under the system, punishment lost its deterrent effect and criminals gained pity in the eyes of black men. He feels that this system was the crowning blow to the faith held by blacks in the integrity of the courts and the fairness of juries.

Historically, the first crime was the crime of the dominant society *against* the black man. He was dehumanized by a totally oppressive system; ruled out of the human family by social theorists, by custom, and by law; excluded from meaningful participation in decisions affecting his life; and socially atomized through assaults on his native culture. The damage inflicted upon blacks by these bestial assaults had, from one point of view, a detrimental effect on their self-esteem, resulting in the citation of various character and behavioral traits among blacks as justification for excluding or criminalizing—the height of racist thinking. But out of this damage also grew a richer self-esteem in direct response to oppression: an irrepressible conviction to rise up and recreate the black culture that was.

Historical Patterns of Crime Among Blacks

The attempt to determine the rates and changes in patterns of crime bears all of the limitations of statistical analysis presented in the literature. Nevertheless, it is the only national data presently available, and attempts to interpret this data still have utility.

The most startling fact about patterns of crime among blacks is that, basically, the predominant pattern is the persistence of crimes against property over the years. This pattern is very consistent with the class-based pattern among all ethnic groups in the United States. Furthermore, the disproportionate rate of crimes against property is found primarily among males. This is reflected in the statistics . . . for the year 1880. The data indicate that of those offenses charged, 57 percent were for crimes against property and 24 percent for crimes against persons. Ninety-three percent of the offenses were charged against males.

The same patterns are repeated in subsequent years. . . . In 1965, assuming the non-white category is composed basically of blacks, the percentage of victimization among blacks in crimes against property (burglary, larceny, and motor vehicle theft) is 75 percent and in crimes against persons (rape, robbery, aggravated assault), 25 percent.

A similar pattern may be seen in . . . victimization data for 1973. However, the [data show no] . . . substantial differences in rates of property crime between blacks and whites. Indeed, if anything, the white rate is somewhat higher than the black rate. Although this may be explained to some extent by the fact that a higher proportion of whites are victimized by blacks for larceny than vice versa . . . the difference is not so great as to explain the high white victimization rates. It is more easily explained by the fact that whites possess more property which can be stolen. This observation serves to highlight the "reality" upon which the social fact of black = criminal has been based. The black rate of violent crime is, however, substantially greater than that for whites; yet it must be emphasized that it still accounts for a minor portion of black crime. The data is also evidence of the historical preoccupation of whites with property—thus they commit more property crimes. The black has suffered not only substantial property deprivation, but personal and cultural destruction; thus his higher rate of crime against persons. The highly intraracial nature of violent personal crime . . . is further support for this view.

Another factor which may affect the race differences in rates of crime against persons may be the selective nature of law enforcement. Numerous studies have demonstrated that blacks get differential treatment from police and from the courts. There is some indication that the police, because of racist views, see certain criminal acts as "normal" for black communities and are slower to respond to calls. Should this be the case, the crime rate in the black community would reflect police practices as well as other factors.

Conclusion

Crime among blacks is a complex *reaction* to oppression. It consists principally of predatory acts against property and it occurs primarily within the black community with blacks as the primary victims. The present-day cry of "crime in the streets" continues a long history of over-reaction by members of the dominant society to an unreal threat. The social scientists and, in this instance, criminologists, have played a major role in perpetuating this fear through theories and research which define the black community as prototypical of the criminal environment. The criminal justice system, and particularly law enforcement, reify these positions through actions based on discretionary powers. The black community itself reflects the exclusion and oppression it has to live under through the bitterness expressed both internally and externally. The violence within the community is an expression of the bitterness turned inward. Racism is the value system on which the entire problem rests. It certainly has economic roots, but it has taken on a reality of its own.

NO EXCUSE FOR CRIME[6]

Except in narrowly specifiable conditions, the law does not see offenders as victims of conditions beyond their control. But criminologists often do. . . .

Consider . . . S. I. Shuman, Professor of Law and Psychiatry at Wayne State University . . . [who] maintains that "if the ghetto victim does what for many such persons is inevitable and is then incarcerated . . . he is in a real sense a political prisoner," because he is punished for "the inevitable consequences of a certain socio-political status." [*Wayne Law Review*, March, 1973] If these consequences were indeed "inevitable," the punishment would be unjust, as Professor Shuman argues. Why, however, would the (unjustly) punished offender become a "political prisoner," as Professor Shuman also claims?

[6] From article by Ernest van den Haag, professor of social philosophy, author of *Punishing Criminals. The Annals.* 423:133–141. Ja. '76. Reprinted from "No Excuse for Crime" by Ernest van den Haag in volume no. 423 of *The Annals of the American Academy of Political and Social Science.* © 1976 by The American Academy of Political and Social Science.

All punishments are imposed, or sanctioned, by the political order which the law articulates. Are all convicts, then, political prisoners? or all those unjustly punished? or all convicts who come from disadvantaged groups? If such a definition were adopted, every convict, all disadvantaged convicts, or everyone unjustly punished would be a political prisoner. "Political prisoner" would become a synonym for "convicted," for "disadvantaged," or for "unjustly punished."

If we want to distinguish between political and other prisoners, a "political prisoner" must be defined as someone imprisoned because he tried to change the political system. The aim of his crime determines whether or not the criminal is political; the offender who intended personal enrichment cannot become a political criminal independently of his actual intent.

Ordinarily, an offender who did not address the political order is not regarded as a political criminal, whether he is a victim of politics or not, whereas an offender whose crime did address the political order is a political criminal, even if he is not a victim of politics. This usage permits a meaningful distinction, which Professor Shuman obliterates by making "political" refer to presumptive causes rather than to overt intentions.

Inevitable Crimes?

Professor Shuman goes on to claim that

arguing that inevitability is too strong a connection between crime and poverty or ghetto existence because not all such persons commit crimes, is rather like arguing that epilepsy or heart attack ought not to excuse because not all epileptics or persons with weak hearts are involved in a chain of events which results in injury.

He adds that "those poverty or ghetto victims who do not commit crimes are extraordinary."

Surely "extraordinary" is wrong here as a statistical generalization: most poor people do not commit crimes;

those who do are extraordinary, not those who don't. Perhaps Professor Shuman means that it takes more resistance within than it does outside the "ghetto" not to commit crimes, which is quite likely. But "inevitability"? Here, the analogy with epilepsy or heart diseases is unpersuasive. Such conditions serve as legal excuses only because they produce seizures beyond the control of the person affected. These seizures are legal excuses only when they are the cause of the crime or injury or of the failure to control it. Otherwise a "weak heart" or an epileptic condition is not an excuse. Thus, poverty could not be an excuse, unless it can be shown to produce seizures beyond their control which cause the poor to commit crimes.

Poverty does not produce such seizures. Nor would poverty deprive the victim, if he were to experience a seizure (of criminality?), of control in the way an epileptic seizure does the epileptic. Poverty affects motivation and increases temptation, as does sexual frustration or, sometimes, marriage—hardly an uncontrollable seizure. To have little or no money makes it tempting to steal; the poverty-stricken person is more tempted than the rich. But a poor person is not shorn of his ability to control temptation. Indeed it is to him that the legal threat is addressed. He is able to respond to it unless he suffers from a specific individual defect or disease which makes him incompetent.

. . . [Shuman] urges that poverty (or slums) should be an excuse since—like power—it leads to crime. Shuman wants to excuse the poor and not the wealthy and powerful, not because, as he suggests, poverty is causally more related to crime than wealth; rather, he sees deprivation as morally unjust and painful, and power and wealth as morally undeserved and pleasant, wherefore he wants to excuse the poor and punish the wealthy. He is morally prejudiced against those corrupted by undeserved wealth—whom he gives no sign of excusing—and in favor of those corrupted by unjust deprivation.

The generosity of his prejudice leads Shuman to overlook a logical error in his argument. In some sense, everybody is what he is, and does what he does, as a result of his genetic inheritance and the influence of his environment—poverty or wealth or power—that interacted with his genetic inheritance and produced him and his conduct. This is no more the case for the poor than for the rich, for criminals than for noncriminals. However, there is no reason to believe that, except in individual cases (which require specific demonstration), genetics, or the environment, so compel actions that the actor must be excused because he could not be expected to control them.

Unless none of us is responsible for what he does, it would have to be shown why criminals, or why poor criminals, are less able to control their conduct and therefore less responsible than others. This cannot be shown by saying that they are a product of the conditions they live in. We all are. Nor can nonresponsibility be claimed by showing that their living conditions are more criminogenic than others. Greater temptation does not excuse from responsibility or make punishment unjust. The law, in attempting to mete out equal punishment, does not assume equal temptation.

VI. SOCIETY'S RESPONSE: CRIMINAL JUSTICE

EDITOR'S INTRODUCTION

As the rate of crime skyrocketed during the last decade, many Americans lost faith in the idea of winning a "war on crime" by fighting crime's causes. Rehabilitation—helping a criminal "go straight"—became an unpopular goal. No method seemed to work, in any case. President Johnson's War on Poverty failed to conquer poverty or reduce the amount of crime committed by poor people.

Thus, those looking for a way to control crime shifted their attention to the criminal justice system—the police, the courts, and the prisons. During the 1970s, the federal government poured millions of dollars into the search for more efficient ways to police the streets. Millions more were invested in projects to streamline the courts, and in the building of more prisons to house an increasing number of prisoners.

In this section's first article, Gerald M. Caplan, former director of the National Institute of Law Enforcement and Criminal Justice, explains why the government's efforts are likely to produce few quick gains. The second article details the results of a federal study of police efficiency, showing that, all too often, sloppy police procedures keep criminal charges from sticking.

The nation's federal, state, and local courts have been assailed by many critics. Much of the criticism is justified: court calendars are clogged, politically appointed judges are sometimes unqualified or lazy or both, and sentencing is not uniform from court to court.

Still, the court system works, thanks in large part to

dedicated judges like Harold Rothwax, profiled here by
Loudon Wainwright, who spent some time watching Judge
Rothwax in action. Wainwright's article presents a close-up
of the inner workings of a criminal court.

In the next piece, Charles E. Silberman, author of the
book *Criminal Violence, Criminal Justice,* delivers his ver-
dict on the nation's criminal courts. "What is remarkable,"
he says, "is not how badly, but how well, most criminal
courts work." The trouble, he says, is one of image: few
courts *appear* to do justice, and so they rarely encourage
respect for the law.

James Q. Wilson, a professor of government at Harvard
University, takes us on a tour of the nation's prisons. Since
repeaters commit most crimes, Wilson advocates reducing
crime by keeping habitual offenders behind bars, where they
cannot prey on society. Wilson is in favor of fixed sentences,
too, instead of indeterminate sentences—sentences that end
when a parole board determines that a prisoner has been
rehabilitated.

The debate over fixed prison-sentencing is the focus of
the volume's final selection, by Burton Wolfe, a writer who
specializes in legal subjects. Relying on the example of
Willie Spann, the nephew of President Jimmy Carter, Mr.
Wolfe makes a plea for flexible sentencing and individualized treatment as the best hope for criminal rehabilitation.

WHY GOVERNMENT ALONE
CAN'T END THE CRIME WAVE[1]

Reprinted from *U.S. News and World Report*

In the past four years, the Federal Government has spent
about 100 million dollars on research into crime. The results have been disappointing in that we have not learned
how to reduce crime, but rewarding in that we have been
able to dispel a number of myths. Here are some examples:

[1] Article based on an interview with Gerald M. Caplan, former director of the
National Institute of Law Enforcement and Criminal Justice. *U.S. News & World
Report.* 82:82. Ap. 11, '77.

Myth No. 1: Government can eliminate crime. We have learned that the conditions that really make a difference in crime control lie largely outside governmental authority—in such areas as child rearing, family stability and transmission of values.

Thus the ability of government—federal, state or local—to do something about crime is far less than we thought back in 1965, when the Federal Government launched its war on crime. For instance, there is no research to support the view that crime could be dramatically reduced by some specific governmental action—such as an antipoverty program or a massive employment program—though undoubtedly benefits would accrue.

These programs have to carry their own justification.

Myth No. 2: More money for police should be a priority. It is clear that in our large cities the prosecutors, the judges and the jailers are unable to handle the volume of arrests that the police make.

Our first priority should be to make our courts more efficient—to drive home the point that they must modernize, so that they can process serious offenders on the charges for which they were arrested without being dependent on plea bargaining. Until we confront this problem, it doesn't make sense to hire more police officers. Police performance is already excessive in terms of the capacity of the rest of the criminal-justice system.

Myth No. 3: Technology is the answer. We have spent about 35 million dollars on equipment development, and while there have been some exciting discoveries—for example, the new police lightweight body armor is a lifesaver—by and large, the Government investment in hardware has not borne fruit. Our over-all experience is that technology will not contribute significantly to reducing crime.

Myth No. 4: Flood an area with police, and you will cut crime. Our best evidence suggests that the number of police patrolling a given area doesn't have much impact on crime.

In Kansas City, researchers studied three areas: one

saturated with police; another where there was a normal number of police patrols, and a third in which police patrol was entirely eliminated, with officers responding only when called. There was no difference in reported crime in the three areas. Although we have long assumed that police presence in a given area works to prevent crime, this study suggests that that assumption is challengeable.

Myth No. 5: The quicker the response, the more likely it is that police will catch criminals. In the last 10 years, we've made dramatic progress in developing modern communication systems. More vehicles and more police are on the streets. Police can respond to a call with great rapidity—often in a matter of minutes. *But* we have recently uncovered another very important problem that prevents police response time from being central to crime reduction:

Citizens often delay calling the police following a crime. As many as two-thirds of all crime victims call somebody or talk to another person before they call the police. Unless we can get citizens to call the police quickly, quick response doesn't make any difference.

Myth No. 6: Drug addicts turn to crime to support their habit. Reasoning from the fact that a large number of criminals use heroin, we leaped to the conclusion that those users became criminals to get money for drugs. The assumption cannot be proved.

In fact, many offenders—just how many is unclear—became criminals first and users second. If they weren't stealing to buy drugs, many would be stealing to acquire other things they want.

Myth No. 7: It is detectives who solve most crimes. This myth has been fed on a preposterous diet of TV shows and movies where the detective always catches the criminal.

But an Institute-sponsored study on detectives suggests that they don't solve that many crimes. In fact, unless the victim or witness at the scene of the crime can give some major clue to the suspect's identity, a detective is not likely to turn it up on his own.

A patrolman on the scene would often do as well. Our

study suggests that effectiveness would not be impaired if the number of detectives were reduced by half, and the remaining half deployed more productively.

Research characteristically raises at least as many questions as it answers—and often many more. It is a slow, painstaking, cumulative process. Should Government continue to sponsor research on crime control? Of course—but not in the hope that research will reduce crime overnight, or even over the next five or 10 years, but simply because it is a sensible way to acquire much-needed new knowledge about a very serious problem.

Perhaps the most important thing we have learned in the last few years is that crime is not the kind of problem that is amenable to breakthrough—as in health, with the Salk vaccine, or the technology that put a man on the moon. It is a problem we will be picking away at for a long time to come, and with luck, there should be a little bit of progress here and a little bit there. Cumulatively it may add up to the kind of knowledge and programs that will have a major impact on our crime problem. That is our hope.

MAKING THE PINCH STING[2]

A policeman collars a mugger on a busy downtown street, but in his haste to make the arrest he forgets to take the names of any witnesses. A burglar is nabbed just as he is leaving the scene of the crime, but while the case against him seems powerful, his loot somehow gets lost in the labyrinth of police headquarters, and he must be set free. A woman catches a second-story man in her house, engages him in conversation, gives him a drink to get his fingerprints. When he flees she calls the police, who refuse to dust the glass for prints because "it's too much trouble."

[2] Article entitled "The Pinch Must Really Sting." *Time.* 110:59–60. S. 26, '77. Reprinted by permission from *Time,* The Weekly Newsmagazine; Copyright Time Inc. 1977.

Completing their "investigation," they leave the flabber-gasted householder to file their report.

These cases, some real, some hypothetical, illustrate a problem that is increasingly distressing prosecutors, judges and the general public. In the battle against crime, police are making more arrests than ever, but the number of convictions is apparently failing to keep pace. According to a major study released this week by the Washington-based Institute for Law and Social Research, more than half the felony arrests were either rejected by prosecutors—who found the evidence too flimsy to bring to court—or subse-quently dismissed by judges for similar reasons.

Undertaken with the help of a grant from the Justice Department's Law Enforcement Assistance Administration, the study, concentrating on Washington, D.C., examined arrest and conviction records compiled by police in the course of a single year. The statistics, which were supported by similar findings in five other urban areas—Los Angeles and San Diego counties, Baltimore, Detroit and Chicago—told an abysmal story. In 1974 Washington's metropolitan police made more than 17,000 arrests for felonies and serious misdemeanors by adults. Yet prosecutors found more than half the cases so flimsy they refused to press charges. Judges tossed out an additional 8%, and in 6% there was no action at all because the defendants simply vanished. The upshot: only 33% of those arrested were ever brought to court for plea or trial. The report acknowledges that factors in the poor conviction record may include the shortage of policemen and such restrictions on police power as the still controversial Miranda rule, which re-quires the arresting officer to inform the suspect of his rights to counsel and to remain silent. But it puts the essential blame on the police themselves, especially for what the study asserts is an obsession with the idea of measuring crime-fighting efficiency only by the number of arrests they make. This policy, described by outgoing FBI Director Clarence Kelley in his foreword as "a perspective that does not extend beyond arrest," produces repercussions all the way down to the beat.

Realizing that making arrests can be a sure way to impress department brass and win promotion, cops grab all the "perpetrators" they can put the arm on, but in their eagerness may neglect rudimentary procedures for gathering proof of the crime that will stand up well in court. With predictable results. In the course of a year, 31% of the Washington cops who made arrests produced no convictions whatsoever.

Police generally deny any departmental obsession with arrest records. They say they are forced into what appears to be an arrest numbers game by the rising crime rate. They also point out that dealing with criminals is complicated and dangerous, and argue that even if an aggressive arrest policy does not always lead to convictions, it has a deterring effect on crime. The Washington study sharply disagrees with this view. The number of suspects arrested, rather than convicted, it contends, not only has little effect on crime but actually undermines the law by making it "difficult for many persons to see how justice is done."

As a remedy, the report urges different training for police, as well as a new reward system that will encourage officers to make "better" arrests. It cites, for example, a recent collaborative experiment in which Washington police and a team of prosecutors combined forces to instruct officers in such elementary matters as interviewing witnesses, verifying the accuracy of their information and advising them on what is expected of a witness in court. The report praises imaginative crime-control tactics like Washington's Operation Sting, in which phony fences were set up to receive stolen goods while officials secretly photographed and recorded the transactions to provide airtight evidence. Such operations, now being carried on in several cities, apparently work quite well. When Washington police took the trouble to produce tangible evidence and reliable witnesses, convictions in robbery arrests went up 60%, in other violent crimes 33% and in crimes against property 36%. The study also reveals another provocative statistic to prove that conviction rates are primarily determined by police procedures. In the cases studied, more than 50% of those arrests that resulted in conviction were regularly made by a handful of skillful officers.

A DAY IN A CROWDED COURT[3]

Seated behind an elevated desk in the high-ceilinged courtroom, Judge Harold Rothwax does not look at all pleased. His broad face, an appealing face with something of the lumpy quality of an old prizefighter's, is set and pale, and his head is pulled down between his shoulders. The two lawyers before him—a young assistant district attorney clutching a confusion of documents and a defense counsel whose brown toupee gleams in contrast to his own dull sideburns—place their hands on the massive desk and seem to brace themselves against his next words. A few spectators stare from the high-backed wooden benches, and in the well of the court, the clerks and uniformed officers are still.

At a table perhaps 20 feet from the judge and behind the lawyers, the defendant stands waiting. He is a handsome white man in his early thirties, and his face above the light turtleneck projects a kind of distaste, as if his straight nose were picking up bad odors at this tawdry proceeding. But he has been in such surroundings many times before. As his record attests, he is a specialist in burglarizing the rooms of first-class hotels, and he often carries a gun to impress anyone unfortunate enough to discover him. He is, in short, a dangerous thief whose devotion to his work led most recently to his capture on one job while he was out on bail after another. He uses different names for different occasions, and he is in bad trouble this morning.

"Tell the defendant," says Judge Rothwax to the defense attorney, in a voice that cannot be heard beyond his

[3] Article entitled "Making Things Happen: The Genius of Harold Rothwax," by Loudon Wainwright, freelance writer. © Saturday Review. 5:14–17. Je. 10, '78. All rights reserved.

desk, "that this is the last day for three and a half to seven. After this, it goes up. If he's going to take the offer, he has to decide now. If he doesn't take it, he's going to trial. We've had enough of this delay. Either he takes the plea, or we set a trial date *today*."

The lawyer looks at the judge for a moment without speaking and then turns and walks back to his client. It is clear that Rothwax is not going to tolerate further stalling. The defendant either must plead guilty to the reduced burglary charge offered by the district attorney—for which Rothwax had earlier indicated he would hand down a sentence of no more than three and a half to seven years in prison—or must prepare to go to trial. Then if a jury convicts him on the original charge (and the prosecution's case seems very good), the trial judge will surely give him a much heavier sentence. And if the defendant wants to delay now and enter a plea later, to avoid trial, the bargain offered today will be unavailable. This is the hard moment of truth in the plea-bargaining process for the handsome burglar, and his face, empty now of any disdain, is taut and angry. He speaks in a rapid whisper to his attorney, stares at Rothwax, shrugs and whispers to his lawyer again.

The lawyer comes back to the bench. "This guy is crazy," he says to Rothwax. "We'll go to trial."

"All right, gentlemen," the judge says briskly. "Let's settle on a date certain for trial."

"Judge, I'd like to be relieved of this case," says the defense lawyer. "This guy won't listen."

Rothwax shakes his head. "No," he replies. "You're the fourth lawyer he's had. That's enough. Let's pick a trial date." It is clear that there is no more room for discussion on this matter. A day two weeks later is selected. The defendant is taken out of the courtroom and back into detention. His case, of course, may still never go to trial, but it has been brought one step closer, largely because of pressure brought by Judge Rothwax. The calendar proceeds.

At forty-seven, Harold Rothwax is a most effective judge not just because of his impressive qualities of intellect, fairness, and knowledge of the criminal law but also because of his rare ability to keep cases moving toward final disposition in a terribly overburdened court system. Nearly 100,000 cases a year come before the New York City criminal court in Manhattan alone, and 5,000 of these result in felony indictments that go on to a higher court. Rothwax is actually a judge of the lower court, but his skills have caused his judicial bosses to place him on the higher bench, as an acting justice of the state supreme court. There he can bring his truly formidable energy and determination to the prompt settlement of more serious cases, involving more complex issues of the law.

Rothwax works in what is called a "calendar part" of the court, a place where many cases are brought before the judge each day. His court is quite unlike the trial parts—which most people think of in connection with criminal justice—where judges preside over one jury trial after another. Different courts call for different techniques of operation, and although Rothwax likes to conduct trials, he is particularly good at the fast-paced, detailed work of running a calendar part, where expert trial judges often get hopelessly bogged down. In Rothwax's court, a succession of matters involving all sorts of serious crimes and alleged criminals, both in and out of jail, are paraded before him. The cases are generally not new, that is, they have been in the court system for some time—several months, even a year —and it is Rothwax's job to push them along toward a solution.

To do this often requires a varying mixture of ingenuity, bluntness, and tact, a blend the judge achieves with remarkable success. He accomplishes the task too with less of a display of his often-raw nerve endings than occasionally bloomed when he was in the lower court. There, for more than three years he dealt with as many as 80 cases a day. Now, in the relative calm of the state supreme court, he seldom hears more than 25. Unlike the judges in some courts who seem almost helpless figures in chaotic charades of justice, Rothwax quite literally dominates the proceed-

ings before him. He seems always in charge, and function-
aries of all sorts tiptoe around him with care, not wanting
to draw his pained look or sharp comment. The judge runs
a tight courtroom—he describes the ideal as "a quiet courtroom, a dignified courtroom, in which you seem to be
seeking truth in a careful, responsible way"—and everybody
knows it.

While he is aware of the commanding image he cuts—
and naturally takes some pleasure in it—Rothwax under-
stands the limits of his job. "The feeling," he says during a
recess in his chambers, "that a judge is an all-powerful
figure can only be held by someone who's never been in the
court system. A good part of a judge's function is that of
a traffic manager, a manager who tries to see that a great
number of things come together at the same time so that
something can happen with the case. But even the best judge
is constantly frustrated by his inability to make these things
happen. Extraordinary coordination between all sorts of
people and agencies is required before anything can take
place.

"Still," Rothwax goes on, "I try to communicate that
I am determined that these things will happen, that I
expect they will happen, and that they are going to happen.
I try to convey the impression that I will not greet kindly
anyone's failure to do his part in the system." To convey
this impression requires that Rothwax be prepared at all
times to insist on prompt, sensible, and orderly work per-
formances by clerks, bailiffs, corrections officers (who produce the jailed defendants), probation officers, police officers, translators, court stenographers, representatives of
various rehabilitation services, and especially by the lawyers for both the people and the defendant. "The impulse
of a good calendar judge," he explains, "is to get the case
resolved and out of the system at the earliest possible moment. But complicated procedures must be correctly followed. So the judge spends a good deal of time making sure
that both sides are doing what they ought to be doing.
He spends a lot of time banging heads."

Rothwax is conspicuously well qualified to do just that. After six years as an aggressive and imaginative defense attorney for New York's Legal Aid Society, he left that job to become director of legal services for the big urban agency Mobilization for Youth, and he has been a professor at Columbia Law School since 1970. Just months before Mayor John Lindsay appointed him to the criminal court in that year, Rothwax wrote a report on the court that included evaluations of the qualifications of the judges sitting there. It was remarkable for its blunt candor about virtually everyone who was working in the criminal justice system.

"The judges and the prosecutors," he wrote, "are often experienced, but they usually are poorly trained for the position they occupy. They are 'ring wise' but either unaware [of] or indifferent to the larger human and social implications about how well the court system performs; they often point to its failures to explain their own shortcomings." Rothwax characterized the poor quality of appointments to the criminal bench as "pervasive and devastating" and went on to comment that there existed "a failure of will and imagination, a lack of coordination and an absence of spirit on the parts of the administrators of the court, the district attorneys, and the Legal Aid Society." Little escaped his scathing notice, and he got appointed as a judge in spite of the fact that he had also characterized members of the mayor's screening committee as "estimable and honorable men" who had "consciously approved [judicial candidates] whom they know to be unacceptable."

Seven years on the bench have mellowed Rothwax somewhat and have made him a little more patient with the uneven performance of the professionals who appear before him. But he is still fierce in the battle against the crushing volume of cases.

"A calendar judge," he says, "is not passive. He does not take frustration easily. If I have been promised the minutes of an earlier hearing and then am told they are not ready at the appointed time, I do not simply accept the bad news. I pursue the matter. I find out why they are not ready. I

say I want those minutes done as soon as possible—I want
them the next day. And I make the lawyers pursue it. If
the prosecutor tells me that his police officer, the man who
arrested the defendant, is on vacation, I want to know why
he hasn't anticipated this, why he didn't know about the
vacation schedule from the very start of the case. If this is
a case we simply must move, I say let's find out where the
officer is on vacation and let's bring him in."

Being a good calendar judge involves more than efficient
traffic management. Much depends on a judge's ability to
bring both sides to an agreement, an agreement whose central condition is that the defendant plead guilty without demanding his right to a trial. This, of course, is plea-
bargaining, and in New York State, judges can actively
participate in the process. In the federal courts, as in the
courts of most of the other states, judges can only ratify
agreements between the prosecutor and the defense. But no
matter what the judge's role, it is a vital part of the criminal
justice process, and without it, the courts simply could not
function.

About his role in plea-bargaining, Rothwax stresses the
importance of proper evaluation. "I must determine," he
says, "the value of each case, how it is ultimately going to
come out if the defendant decides to test the system and go
to trial.

"Knowing the worth of a case," he continues, "is a com-
pound of many things, of getting the answers to many questions. From the prosecutor's point of view, is this a strong
case? Can he actually prove it? Can he get all his evidence
in—or has some been illegally obtained?

"Then there are the personalities involved. What kind
of lawyers am I dealing with? Is this prosecutor a good trial
lawyer who is willing, even anxious, to take this case all the
way? Or is he a guy who is gun-shy about trials and would
prefer some disposition short of that? Is this a defense attorney who is effective and dedicated? Is he knowledgeable
in the law? Or is he lazy?

"In the case of a serious crime where the defendant has

other felony convictions, the district attorney holds the bargaining leverage. He can make an offer and stick to it, and the law involving multiple felonies gives me no scope in sentencing. But most often this is not the case. The mandatory sentencing provisions do not apply, and there are choices possible. The DA may say that he will not make a plea offer lower than a B felony [an A is the most serious]. The defense attorney may respond that he doesn't care about labels—B, C, D—that all he is concerned with is the amount of time I'm going to give his client. And with a B felony, I have a scope of anywhere from three years to twenty-five years. We can move toward an agreement.

"In one case I had recently," the judge continues, "the defendant was a burglar of long experience. The case was a strong one: The defendant had been found in the complainant's bed—where he had crawled in great pain after falling from the penthouse roof in the course of the burglary and breaking both legs.

"The assistant DA had the case ready to go to trial and would take no plea less than a C felony. Because the guy was a prior felon, I had no discretion in sentencing and would have to give him from three to six years in prison. Under the circumstances, I thought a sentence of two to four years would be sufficient. I felt the breaking of his legs had effected some kind of change within him. And he had reached the age of forty, well past the peak for a cat burglar. Aging is the one sure cure we have for crime.

"But the young DA would not reduce the charge," Rothwax explains, "and because she was relatively inexperienced, I decided to take it up with her boss, who was trying a case on another floor of the courthouse. I got up off the bench, took both lawyers, and went and found this guy. He was standing out in the hallway. The jury in his case was out—was hanging, in fact—and we all talked it over for about half an hour. It surely helped that the boss's jury was hung. I was able to point to his own situation and say, 'Look, here's a case you thought was strong. You were sure you could win. And the jury is hanging because one juror refuses to deliberate with the others. Now in this other matter where I think two to four years would be enough, nobody was hurt except the burglar, and the complainant is a tax fugitive in Europe. The case will have to be proved circumstantially. If this guy goes to trial, you can't tell what will happen. We're not seers. But with the two to four sentence on the reduced charge, you're getting a certain disposition with a significant punishment.' I urged him to accept that, and he did."

The judge continues more generally on the uses of plea-bargaining. "A lot of people criticize it as being weighted for the defendant," he says, "but in my view, plea-bargaining is neutral, depending on the way people deal with it. If both sides are conscientious, well informed, well prepared, if the plea-bargain reflects the seriousness of the charge and the background of the defendant, it can be very good. If on the other hand it has too great a dependence on extraneous factors—the personalities of the attorneys, the unavailability of trial parts or of witnesses—it can be bad. But it lends certainty, promptness, and finality to a process that otherwise often doesn't have it. As I keep telling attorneys: Certainty is preferable to severity as long as the sentence we're imposing is a reasonable one."

Like the other judges in New York's criminal court, Harold Rothwax takes his turn at weekend duty in the crowded arraignment part, the lowest court in the system. This is where, seven days a week, cases of all sorts are first brought; where defendants are charged; where cases are dismissed, held over for the grand jury, or assigned to another part; where bail is fixed; where the judge often seeks immediate solutions to minor matters and imposes short jail sentences or modest fines. This is the court where the feel and smell of pain, rage, sorrow, poverty, and the rank city are the strongest. It is the pit of urban justice; the room is tense with the lingering reverberations of acts that took place only yesterday.

Rothwax has a long familiarity with this place, both as a judge and as a defense attorney, and on a recent Sunday he managed the calendar with an almost surgical dexterity, flipping fast through the papers handed to him, summoning the lawyers to whispered bench conferences, instructing the "bridgeman"—who calls defendants before the bench—which case he wanted to hear next, asking a young defendant if he understood what his lawyer had just told him about the probable consequences of a plea being offered. Rothwax dealt with matters involving assault, car theft, prostitution, possession of a weapon, robbery, drugs (a relatively "heavy" case in which the defendants had been caught with heroin worth about $25,000 on the street), impersonation of a police officer. He kept it all moving easily.

In his chambers during a recess, he smoked a cigar and relaxed. He wished aloud that he'd ridden his bike the five miles down to court, as he usually does when it isn't raining hard or snowing. He wondered if his wife and two small children would come down to join him for dinner at a Chinese restaurant near the courthouse. Then he got back to the subject of court business and told the story of a man who had recently appeared before him on a homicide charge that was nearly 10 years old. When the murder had occurred, the defendant had been a sick man, an alcoholic who often blacked out. He had hit another man over the head in the course of a holdup and had killed him. Then he had fled to Arkansas, where he got a job, stopped drinking, got married and had a child, and lived entirely peacefully and undetected for many years.

Last Christmas, as the judge told it, the man, unable to live with his conscience any longer, walked into a local police station and confessed to the crime. Brought back to New York, he eventually appeared before Rothwax, who reviewed the record, studied the voluminous reports from social workers and psychiatrists, pondered the last blameless years of the defendant's life, and deliberated about the right way to dispose of the case. Eventually, all the parties agreed to a solution: The man pleaded guilty to manslaughter in the second degree, was given a deferred sentence, and was allowed to go back on probation to his family in Arkansas. This happy and humane result was obviously a source of satisfaction to the judge.

Such outcomes affirm his good feelings about his job. "I think judging is terrific in a way," he said. "You're always in the process of learning, you're always drinking it in, and you're never sated. I'm independent, nobody tells me what to do. My job is to know the law and to understand the law—to do the right thing."

But not many of the cases Harold Rothwax hears work out like the Arkansas case, and the recollection of the others upsets him. "At times, a judge can read a presentence report and cry," he said. "I mean literally cry. You read that this kid's parents beat him brutally when he was young and they broke his arm and he fell on his head and they left him and they were drunkards and addicts and he grew up with an aunt who ran a whorehouse and he was beaten and thrown out of the house and there was endless noise and he had to share a bedroom with fourteen others and there was one bed and it was cold in the winter and hot in the summer and there was no food and he never felt loved, wanted, desired, needed, esteemed. You read this kind of a thing, and you wonder at the capacity of human beings to survive.

"How does this guy go on? How does he get dressed in the morning? How does he function—even as a criminal? And the saddest thing about all this is that now you've got a twenty-five-year-old guy who's acting out on the world the way the world has acted out on him. While your heart can cry for him, you know there's no way you're going to change him, and you know that he poses a singular threat to the kinds of decency and peacefulness you want in the world. Maybe there'll be intervals, but by and large that's what it's going to be: He's going to act out his rage on others a good deal of the time when we're silly enough to let him go.

"Isn't that a terrible judgment?" Rothwax asked, as the bridgeman signaled it was time to get going with the calendar again. "How do you live with that? Obviously there's guilt for it. And it's not only the guilt of the parents and the guilt of the society. But in a way you have to desentimentalize that kind of a thing, you have to become a little unfeeling. It seems to me that the question for the judge in this situation is: Is there any way we can reconcile this individual with his society? And if that conclusion in an unsentimental way is no, then this guy has got to go to jail." Rothwax rose and brushed a cigar ash from the front of his black robe. Then as the bridgeman called for order, the judge hurried back into the crowded court.

THE CRITICS ARE WRONG[4]

Criminal courts are on trial, charged with failing to protect the American people against criminal violence. Some critics attribute the failure to a gross shortage of resources that forces prosecutors and judges to indulge in plea-bargaining, offering serious criminals a mild penalty in return for a guilty plea.

Others put the blame on the Warren Court's rulings protecting the rights of the accused, which force prosecutors and police to release, and judges to acquit, large numbers of patently guilty offenders.

Still others believe the major flaw to be the arbitrary and capricious nature of criminal sentencing, which leads to wide disparities in the punishments meted out to offenders guilty of the same crime.

Whatever their emphasis, the critics agree that the courts fail to administer swift, certain and equitable punishment, and that this failure encourages criminal violence.

The critics are wrong—wrong in the "facts" they cite, wrong in the way they interpret them, and wrong in the conclusions they draw and the remedies they propose.

[4] From "Justice," article by Charles E. Silberman, director of the Study of Law and Justice, a Ford Foundation research project and author of *Criminal Violence, Criminal Justice*. New York *Times*. p 45. N. 7, '78. © 1978 by The New York Times Company. Reprinted by permission.

□ It is not true that the police or the courts have been handcuffed by the rulings of the Warren Court. Only a handful of criminals escape arrest, conviction or punishment because of exclusionary rules, search-and-seizure laws, and other "technicalities" designed to protect defendants' rights.

□ It is not true that the courts are more lenient than they used to be. A larger proportion of arrested felons are incarcerated now than in the 1920's, when the accused had far fewer protections.

□ It is not true that disparate sentencing practices undermine the deterrent power of the criminal law. Within any single court system, the great majority of sentences— on the order of 85 per cent—follow informal norms and can be predicted if one knows the nature of the offense and of the offender's prior record.

□ It is not true that plea-bargaining distorts the judicial process. It is the principal means by which prosecutors and judges make the punishment fit the crime: Plea-bargaining occurs as frequently in rural areas as in big cities and has been the dominant means of settling criminal cases for the last century. (Attempts to ban plea-bargaining merely shift it to some other, less visible, part of the system.)

□ Most important, it is not true that significant numbers of guilty offenders escape punishment in criminal court. When charges are dropped, it usually is because the victim refuses to press charges, because a key witness declines to cooperate, or because the prosecutor doubts the defendant's guilt or lacks the evidence needed to sustain a conviction.

When one examines what actually happens, in short, what is remarkable is not how badly, but how well, most criminal courts work. They generally do an effective job of separating the guilty from the innocent; most of those who should be convicted are convicted, and most of those who should be punished are punished. Thus, there is no reason to believe that the reforms now being proposed— repealing the exclusionary rule, mandating prison terms for dangerous criminals, forbidding plea-bargaining, or reducing or eliminating judges' and parole boards' discretion —would bring about any noticeable reduction in criminal violence.

This is not to suggest that we live in the best of all possible worlds; far from it. It is to argue that what is wrong with the judicial process is less the results it produces than the means by which it produces them. As the old maxim has it, the appearance of justice is as important as justice itself. Most criminal courts *do* do justice; almost none of them *appears* to do justice. Instead, they convey an aura of injustice, undermining respect for law by the shabby, haphazard, and surly way in which they are run.

In any society, respect for law is a more effective instrument of social control than fear of punishment. If the criminal courts are to contribute to a reduction in criminal violence, it will not be by stuffing more people into already overcrowded prisons and jails; it will be by encouraging respect for law—by persuading people to obey the law because it is the law. For that to happen, the courts will have to become models of due process—living demonstrations that fairness and justice are possible, that human beings can be treated with decency and concern.

WHO IS IN PRISON?[5]

Prisons are usually newsworthy only when their inmates riot, but of late they have become the focus of more general, and on the whole more constructive, attention. The revival of interest in the deterrent effects of the criminal-justice system, the spreading "prisoner-rights" movement, the decisions of various federal judges to close (or to threaten to close) various overcrowded or indecent jails and prisons, the sudden increase in the size of the prison population, and the emerging debate over whether new prison construc-

[5] Article by James Q. Wilson, Henry Lee Shattuck Professor of Government at Harvard University, author of *Thinking About Crime*. *Commentary*. 62:55–8. N. '76. Reprinted from *Commentary*, by permission; copyright © 1976 by the American Jewish Committee.

tion is desirable have all combined to thrust a venerable and unpleasant institution onto center stage.

The debate over prisons raises many issues—the length of sentences, the function of parole, the level of amenity, the feasibility of rehabilitation, the rights of inmates—but central to most of these issues are some mundane but rarely examined constraints. If one wishes to award longer sentences to those who now go to prison, or short sentences to a larger fraction of those convicted of a crime, one must find a place to put them. If one wishes to increase the level of amenity, it presumably requires lowering the density of prison populations: it is hard to imagine how to make any institution less brutal if three or four persons are assigned to a cell designed for one, or if persons must sleep in the corridor or on the floor. Among the rights that most inmates certainly cherish is the right not to be abused by fellow prisoners, yet that can scarcely be insured without producing a greater degree of privacy, and accordingly supplying more square feet, for each inmate. In short, the sheer capacity of the prison system will importantly influence what, if anything, can be done toward achieving various objectives.

In general, we do not know what the "capacity" of our prison system is. There are about 400 prisons, 158 community centers and work farms, and 33 other (reception, diagnostic, medical, or classification) facilities operated by the states. Half of all of these are located in the South. These figures, the best available, were compiled by the Census Bureau in January 1974, but that agency admits that there may be more or different institutions—it is hard to be certain what is a distinct facility, some facilities have more than one function, and half of the institutions in one state (Massachusetts) did not even bother to reply to the questionnaire. The survey did not indicate what the "capacity" of each facility was and no survey probably could, inasmuch as many correctional administrators have long since had to put more inmates into a prison than it was designed to receive and in consequence have administratively redefined what constitutes its capacity.

We do know that the great majority of prisoners are in conventional closed prisons, not in work farms or community centers. Though the movement to place more convicted offenders in these "open" facilities has grown of late, less than a tenth of the correctional population is in community centers and less than a seventh on prison farms. Though most inmates are in real prisons, the popular image of these facilities as uniformly ancient and decrepit is not necessarily true. Nearly half of all prisons were built since 1949 and three-fourths were constructed since 1924. There are at least 50 prisons, however, that were built in the 19th century, several around the time of the Civil War.

If we cannot measure the capacity of prisons, we can at least count their populations. Except for the period during and just after World War II, that population has been remarkably stable. There were 180,000 persons in state and federal prisons in 1939, and there were still about that many in prison fifteen years later, in 1954. During the 1950's, a period of relatively stable or only moderately rising crime rates, the prison population went up sharply—from 166,000 in 1950 to 213,000 in 1960. Then, during the 1960's, a period of rapidly increasing crime rates, the prison population actually declined from 213,000 in 1960 to 196,000 in 1970.

Why the prison population should go up when crime is not serious and go down when it has become a national crisis still defies explanation. One possibility is that certain judges came to believe that prison was an inappropriate way to treat criminals—because these facilities did not rehabilitate, or because they were unpleasant places to live, or because prison was generally "illiberal." This explanation is lent plausibility by the fact that many of the largest reductions in state-prison populations during this decade occurred in states, such as New York, Michigan, Pennsylvania, Minnesota, and Hawaii, with a strong tradition of liberal politics and presumably a liberal judiciary. Yet declines also occurred in Mississippi, West Virginia, Georgia, Alabama, Kansas, and Kentucky, hardly hotbeds of leftists.

One of the most intriguing theories devised to explain the relative stability over long periods of time in imprisonment rates is that advanced by Alfred Blumstein, Jacqueline Cohen, and Daniel Nagin of Carnegie-Mellon University. They show that, not only in the United States but in Norway and Canada as well, the imprisonment rate—the number of persons in prison per 100,000 population—is remarkably stable. Between 1930 and 1970 in this country it averaged around 110 with only small variations around this mean (the standard deviation was less than 9). In the late 1930's, the rate went up to abnormally high levels, in the 1940's down to abnormally low ones, in the 1950's it increased, and in the 1960's it decreased. Their theory is that society penalizes less serious offenses at times when serious crime is not a problem and lets off minor offenders when serious crime has become endemic. If murder is relatively uncommon or at least declining in rate (as it was during the 1950's), society will worry more about shoplifting, prostitution, and auto theft. When murder, assault, and robbery are increasing rapidly (as they did in the 1960's), society will ignore the shoplifter and seek—*de facto* if not *de jure*—to decriminalize prostitution.

The theory is quite suggestive, but thus far unproved. Among other difficulties, it does not account for the substantial variation among states in the use of prison. Crime rates during the 1960's were soaring in both Michigan and New Jersey, but whereas the former state reduced its prison population, the latter increased it despite similar rates of population change. Massachusetts officials have long been preoccupied with the dangers of overcrowded prisons and perhaps in consequence of this kept their prison population constant during the 1960's despite a tripling of the serious crime rate. South Carolina, on the other hand, allowed its prison population to rise by more than 30 per cent even though it meant increased overcrowding. For some states, the capacity of the prison system is apparently an important constraint on the sentencing practices of judges, but in other states it is not.

In recent years, the prison population has started to rise again. In early 1976, according to *Corrections* magazine, there were nearly 250,000 persons in prison, the largest number since figures began to be kept. In the Blumstein, *et al.*, theory, this was to be expected—after allowing the imprisonment rate to fall during the 1960's (from 119 per 100,000 in 1960 to 97 per 100,000 in 1970), it was inevitable that pressure to respond to the crime wave would drive it back up to its traditional average of around 110. If that rate is applied to the estimated 1975 total population, it would produce a prison population of 234,000, significantly below the actual figures.

The reasons for the increase above expected levels are not hard to find. The population today is more youthful than at any other time in this century, and since young people are disproportionately criminals, it is not surprising that prisoners are growing in numbers faster than society generally. Furthermore, many of the young offenders who were first convicted in the 1960's are now being convicted for the third or fourth time and as a result can no longer expect to avoid prison through probation or suspended sentences. In addition it is *possible* that judges are becoming more severe, but since we have no national statistics on sentencing that can only be a conjecture.

There is nothing magical about the long-term stability of the imprisonment rate. Society can choose a higher or a lower rate, in part by altering its prison capacity. That can be accomplished by either building more facilities, reducing the sentences of those going to prison, or changing the mix of persons in prison. The first policy results in an absolute increase in prison size, the second permits more persons to be sentenced to prisons despite a constant capacity, and the third permits one to find prison space for increased numbers of more serious offenders.

No accurate national figures exist on changes in total

prison capacity. The federal Bureau of Prisons, which has in confinement about 10 per cent of all prisoners, has, in the last five years opened thirteen new facilities with a total capacity of over 4,000 inmates but still feels that its system is overcrowded by about 5,000 inmates. Among the states, major new building programs are under way or proposed in Florida, Alabama, North Carolina, Ohio, and elsewhere. The National Moratorium on Prison Construction, a lobbying group sponsored by the Unitarian-Universalist Service Association and the National Council on Crime and Delinquency, which opposes prison construction, reports that it has heard of over 500 planned institutions. Whatever the actual figure, it has so far been inadequate to alleviate the severe overcrowding that now exists and that will, almost certainly, become worse.

Because capacity has not kept up with inmates, there has occurred a dramatic shift in the kinds of crimes for which persons go to prison [see Table 1, page 201]. In 1960, the federal Bureau of Prisons counted about 151,000 persons in state prisons. In 1974, the Census Bureau (which has taken over the job of keeping track of prison populations) estimated, on the basis of a survey of about 10,000 inmates, that there were 188,000 persons in state prisons. The increase in size is partly an artifact of who was counted; in 1960, some states gave incomplete or inaccurate figures and persons not in closed prisons were often omitted. In 1974, the coverage was broader and included persons in certain state mental hospitals as well as those on work-release programs and in community centers. Because the figures are not entirely reliable, only gross differences should be noted. The striking finding is that prison is increasingly reserved for only the most serious offenders. Persons convicted of homicide, robbery, and assault made up one-third of the state-prison population in 1960 but nearly half in 1974. There are nearly twice as many murderers in prison today as in 1960 and 70 per cent more robbers. By contrast, the numbers of burglars, thieves, and auto thieves in prison has actually declined—from about 55,300 in 1960 to about 49,200 in 1974. (During this period, the reported rate of these crimes increased more than fourfold.)

TABLE 1

Offenses for Which Adult Inmates Were Sentenced to State Prisons

Offense	1960	1974
Homicide	18,538	34,000
Robbery	24,627	42,400
Assault	7,739	9,000
Burglary	35,418	33,800
Larceny	14,284	12,200
Auto theft	5,633	3,200
Embezzlement, fraud, forgery	15,633	8,100
Sex (including rape)	12,656	11,700
Drugs	8,030	18,700
Other	8,144	14,400
TOTAL	150,702	187,500

Some have argued that we do not need more prisons because the ones we have are crowded with persons serving sentences for various "victimless" crimes. This was not true in 1960 and it is not true today. Only 10 per cent of the 1974 inmates were serving sentences for drug offenses and only one per cent for sex offenses other than forcible rape. Of the drug offenders, nearly half were serving time for trafficking in hard drugs, such as heroin. Thus, only 6 per cent of the inmates were doing time for merely possessing a drug or trafficking in marijuana. The number of persons in prison for gambling is not reported, but could not exceed one per cent.

Others have argued that prison should be reserved for repeat offenders and not used for persons convicted for the first time. By and large, that is already the case. Less than one per cent of the inmates had never been sentenced before; 28 per cent had served four or more prior sentences.

Prison inmates are, as one would expect, disproportionately drawn from among the poorly educated and those with low income. About half are black (in 1960 only a third were) and most never finished high school. Contrary to what one might suppose, inmates are not typically unemployed during the month preceding their arrest. Two-thirds were employed, and almost all of these said they were employed full time. Of those unemployed, the majority said they had not been looking for work and did not want work.

The other way society can alter its prison capacity is by changing the amount of time the average inmate serves. The shorter that period, the more space each year for additional inmates. Unfortunately, no good figures are available on time served by inmates of all state prisons. We do have such data for certain jurisdictions, however, and we can make an estimate of it for prisons generally. Overall, the length of time served in prison seems to have remained pretty much the same over the last decades or so: for the average inmate, about two years (he may be sentenced to much longer terms, but offenders are actually incarcerated for no more than one-third to one-half of their nominal sentences). This would suggest that nothing has changed. But that is a mistaken inference. Recall that the average prisoner is more likely today to be a murderer or robber and much less likely to be a burglar or auto thief. If time served has remained constant, it can only mean the time served in prison for more serious offenses, such as murder and robbery, has become less.

It is not clear, of course, whether any changes in time served were the result of judicial decisions. Other agencies, such as parole boards, can and do decide how long a person will stay in prison whatever the initial sentence. How this has changed is vividly shown by the experience of the federal correctional system. Federal judges, like their state counterparts, sent fewer persons to prison in 1970 than in 1960—30 per cent fewer, as it turns out—despite the rising crime rate. For those they did imprison, however, they issued longer sentences: in 1960, average sentence length was about 27 months, but in 1970 it was over 38 months. At the same time, however, the proportion of the sentence actually served fell—from about 64 per cent in 1960 to 51 per cent in 1970. As a result, the actual time served remained about constant (around a year and a half) despite the fact that federal prisons in 1970 had a larger proportion of inmates who had committed more serious crimes, such as robbery, assault, and firearms-law violations.

In sum, we have adapted to higher crime rates by reducing the proportions of arrested persons going to prison (a pattern that recently may have been reversed), changing the mix of prison populations to emphasize serious over less serious offenders, keeping more or less constant the average amount of time served despite the fact that those in prison are guilty of more serious crimes, and allowing overcrowding to occur in many systems (especially in the South).

From many different, and even competing, perspectives, this has not been a rational response. If you believe that increasing the percentage of convicted offenders who are imprisoned will deter others from committing crimes, then a declining prison population and a declining imprisonment rate are mistakes. If you believe that more serious offenders should be kept off the streets longer, then a constant sentence length at a time when the prison population is coming disproportionately to consist of serious offenders is a mistake. If you believe that prison conditions are inhuman and indecent, then allowing overcrowding to occur in many states makes difficult or impossible the provision of higher levels of privacy and amenity. If you believe that "white-collar" criminals should be given prison sentences more frequently (either to deter others, to exact retribution, or to prevent the burden of prison from falling overwhelmingly on the poor and the black), then maintaining a limited prison capacity is a mistake, because white-collar (and other nonviolent) offenders will inevitably be displaced by blue-collar, violent ones. (Between 1960 and 1970, the number of persons in federal prison who were convicted of income-tax violations, embezzlement, fraud, and forgery declined while the number convicted of robbery increased.)

In short, increasing the capacity of our prison system is consistent with, if not indeed mandated by, a variety of policy goals that are often thought to be in opposition. It is not clear, of course, that merely having more "prisons"— and by that I mean all variety of facilities, community-based as well as maximum-security—will induce judges to use them more, parole boards to leave serious offenders in longer, or wardens to devote more effort to producing decent and humane environments. It would seem, however, that for the nation as a whole, if not for every state, the more or less fixed capacity of our prison system has been allowed to become a major constraint on, or excuse for, sentencing policy. William A. Shaffer of MIT has shown, through a careful analysis of the Massachusetts criminal-justice system, how this constraint operates in practice. In that state, he suggests, the shortage of prison capacity is the critical variable affecting the ability of the system to lower crime rates —much more so than police resources or court decisions.

The cities and states, of course, are often pinched for money, in some cases led by officials who believe that only harsh correctional systems are of any value, and usually caught in the middle between citizen groups that want less crime and those that want to block the construction of new prisons. The problem will become more acute as prison populations continue to rise, as they have begun to do. I suggest that the next national administration, whether motivated principally by a concern for victims or inmates, has an obligation to examine the federal relationship to the state-prison system and to think seriously about the desirability of supplying both more funds for expansion of that system and higher standards for its operation.

THE CASE OF THE PRESIDENT'S NEPHEW[6]

One day in March 1976, California parole agent Steve Northrup visited a Tenderloin district apartment in San Francisco to check on one of his clients, William Carter Spann—the nephew of President Jimmy Carter.

Thirty-year-old Willie Spann was on parole from a previous sentence involving burglary and violation of probation by possession of an unauthorized weapon. He was living in the apartment with a group of street people: a burglar, a homosexual dope dealer, the dealer's lover, and a mentally disturbed young woman who had been a street-walker for a short time while Willie pimped for her.

Northrup did not know all this, but he saw enough to be worried. He noticed that Willie's eyes looked puffy. He asked to look at Willie's arms. They bore scratches and puncture marks. Northrup escorted Willie from the apartment and locked him up in the San Francisco city jail.

Willie's blood and urine confirmed that he was "under the influence of heroin and amphetamines." Northrup recommended to the California Adult Authority that Willie be returned to prison for at least a 90-day dryout period, if not for treatment of drug abuse (in the California penal system, treatment is as rare as snow in San Francisco). Instead, the authority discharged him. That disposal of the case was followed by a predictable result.

Willie Spann was living on a dosage of heroin and speed that required a daily outlay of $80 to $90. He had no job. Nor had he lived long enough or established enough street connections in San Francisco to become a dealer himself. Nor were friends and relatives giving him any allowance; his uncle, a candidate for president, and his mother, the candidate's sister, had refused to send him a dime, figuring that he would only use it for drugs. Consequently, Willie

[6] From "Liberal Solution Number 1,666,666," article by Burton H. Wolfe, writer specializing in legal subjects, author of *Pileup on Death Row. Juris Doctor.* 7:24+. My. '77. Copyright © 1977 by MBA Communications, Inc. Reprinted by permission.

was obtaining money for his daily drug dose through the only method available to him—theft.

As soon as the adult authority released Willie, he resumed his new career as burglar and armed robber, adopted one month after his previous release from San Quentin. His armed robberies were poorly planned. They included saloons where he was well known. There were witnesses and clues left behind at each robbery. There was, in fact, almost a plea to the authorities—"Come and get me before I do worse." And so they did. It was one of the easiest arrests of the year.

Now it was no longer up to the adult authority. A San Francisco superior court judge sentenced Willie to a term of five years to life. Soon the length of that term may be fixed under a new determinate sentencing law. The governor and legislature of California have offered it as a humanitarian reform of indeterminate sentencing laws, viewed by some as unjust. Under the new law, Willie Spann will have a more definite idea of when he can expect to get out of prison. But not an absolutely definite idea, because scholars and experts are still debating the exact meaning and workings of the new determinate sentencing law. Of course the experts have difficulty even defining the terms used to describe the sentencing laws, since "indeterminate" sentences have fixed limits and "determinate" ones always have some flexibility.

Whatever the meaning, it will not be necessary for anyone to wait until next year for an evaluation of the new law's social worth. In fact, anyone could have made the evaluation two years ago, after the California Supreme Court handed down a decision, known as *In Re Rodriguez,* that amounted to a determinate sentencing law.

In Re Rodriguez, in fact, determined the fate in March 1976 of President Carter's nephew. I know because that's what I found out five months later when I began investigating Willie Spann's past for a series of newspaper and magazine articles. I was disturbed because his parole officer,

Steve Northrup, told me he knew Willie was hooked on drugs and was dangerous to himself and society, and he would either be taken off the streets or there would be serious trouble. That's what Northrup had told the members of the adult authority. But they had acted as though they had not even heard him. I wanted to know why. Northrup suggested I phone Jerry Sims, regional hearing coordinator in the parole revocation division of the adult authority.

"A decision known as *In Re Rodriguez* was handed down last year by the California Supreme Court," Sims explained to me. "It mandates that the adult authority discharge an individual after a certain length of time. It has nothing to do with why [Willie Spann] was caused to come before the adult authority or what the parole agent recommends. It is simply a matter of following the ruling by the Supreme Court that once an individual has been out on the street a certain time, he must be released by the adult authority. SB-42 [Senate Bill 42, which had just been passed by the California legislature] follows the lines of what the adult authority was already doing under *Rodriguez.*"

The new California law curtails the practice of indeterminate sentencing and more rigidly fixes the date by which a prisoner or parolee must be released from custody. Similar changes are being instituted or at least discussed in other states, and the subject has become a fad among politicians, lawyers, and judges who want people to believe that some kind of reform can be wrought by changing from indeterminate to determinate sentencing.

But the trouble with *either* kind of sentencing was described to me 11 years ago by Bill Sands, founder and president of the Seventh Step Foundation, not long before he died of heart disease at the age of 45. Sands, whose original last name was Sewell, was the emotionally disturbed son of a California judge. He committed a few robberies, got caught, and was locked up in San Quentin. There he developed theories about the causes of criminal behavior and what is needed to correct it. These theories were incorporated in *My Shadow Ran Fast,* a best-selling book he wrote about his life, and Seventh Step, the convict self-help organization he created.

Any intelligent, competent, perceptive prison warden, psychologist, psychiatrist, or social worker can look at a convict and tell you when he's ready and when he's not ready to get out [Sands told me one day in a San Francisco hotel where he was attending a criminology conference]. That's the trouble with our sentencing laws, whether they fix a date or let a term run on forever or at the whim of a parole board. They don't take into account individual human differences. They don't allow those who know a convict most intimately to determine when he should and should not get out of the joint, for his own good and for the good of the society.

I can show you a man who's committed a murder, but after a year he's made such a complete turnaround that he's ready to get out of prison, and he can't because his first parole hearing date is another year away. And I can show you another guy who's in for a minor theft, and he's due to get out next week, and he's an absolute homicidal nut who's going to kill somebody if he isn't locked up till he's well. Now, either way you go with these people, you're in real trouble if you don't let them out when their behavior, rather than a sentencing law, tells you they're ready.

That guy who's been in the joint just a year—right now, he still feels positively enough about the outside world, about the system, to believe he can return to it and be a productive part of it. There's nothing further to be gained by keeping him in the joint because he's reached his peak of rehabilitation. There's no farther up he can go.

But he can go down, and he will, even if you keep him just one more year. His frustrations and anger will start to eat away at him. There's a chance he'll come under the influence of antisocial elements who will convince him the system is unjust, and then he becomes a member of the convict culture. Maybe sexual frustration will lead to an affair with another prisoner, and that sets off a whole string of trouble. Or maybe he'll get hold of some dope and use it to ease his anxiety and tension. Whatever he does, the point is that the blind, stupid authorities have pushed him along the path to becoming a more hardened convict, instead of a rehabilitated one, by refusing to let him out when he's ready to go.

Meanwhile, they've let out another guy who's going to come right back next month or next year, this time for a more violent crime, maybe even a murder.

The same principle applies to my recent convict subject, Willie Spann. If judgment had been left to his parole officer, or even a series of lab tests, there would have been a dozen fewer armed robberies in San Francisco during 1976 and maybe two less people shot—not by Willie, but rather his partner in crime, who very nearly killed a saloon worker during one of their holdups.

Try to discuss that with lawyers and judges as they debate the merits and workings of California's and other states' new indeterminate sentencing laws. They don't want to listen. In fact, they almost visibly shudder. Because you are then talking about taking the power to fix or refix offenders' sentences from legislature, judge, and parole authority. You're talking about adopting instead open-ended sentencing that leaves time to be served to the judgment of prison wardens, psychiatrists, counselors, or maybe even the supervised board of convicts and ex-convicts that Bill Sands proposed—on the grounds that only they really know how to judge whether an offender needs freedom or more lockup time. Most judges, lawyers, and politicians would rather avoid that kind of talk.

Nor do most psychiatrists want to hear it. The majority are from Freudian, neo-Freudian, and so-called "dynamic" and "eclectic" schools—all considered "liberal" or "progressive" and "humanitarian." Any psychiatrist who suggests setting up a mental or emotional evaluation system that determines release from prison by qualifying the inmate's state of being is considered at best a behaviorist, at worst a totalitarian. Fears are expressed that incompetent, bureaucracy-oriented, punishment-oriented government psychiatrists and psychologists would stamp or label inmates by various unacceptable categories (as if they don't already) that prevent their ever being released.

Based on the quality of government-employed psychiatrists and psychologists I have observed in the prison system, I cannot say these fears are unwarranted. There is, of course, the alternative of paying psychiatrists and psychologists in private practice to take sufficient time out from

earning $30 to $50 an hour to share the monitoring of inmate mental and emotional condition. Too expensive?
Hardly. What could be more expensive than the system we
have now, which results in 50 to 75 percent of parolees
committing additional crimes and returning to prison?

I want to shout a message into the ears of all lawyers
and judges in this country, however well-intentioned, who
are discussing the improvements or drawbacks of determinate and indeterminate sentencing laws: You are engaging in
self-destructive sophistry and a socially destructive waste
of time. You can fill your meeting or conference rooms with
enough hot air to crack the walls, and it won't make any
difference in the crime and recidivism rates. The passage
of a new determinate sentencing law is liberal solution
number 1,666,666.

The real solution lies in tearing down the prisons, replacing them with small, individualized treatment or rehabilitation centers, and learning from the convicts themselves when they are ready to be returned to the society
at large.

No sophisticated argument over determinate and indeterminate sentencing laws has anything to do with that.

That's the lesson to be learned from the short story
about Willie Spann, the nephew of President Carter, now
serving time at Soledad prison in California. His crimes
might have been prevented, simply by heeding a parole
agent's plea to put his client away for treatment of drug
abuse, instead of releasing his client to comply with an
absurd sentencing law.

BIBLIOGRAPHY

An asterisk (*) preceding a reference indicates that the article or part of it has been reprinted in this book.

BOOKS, PAMPHLETS, AND DOCUMENTS

Clark, Ramsey. Crime in America: observations on its nature, causes, prevention and control. Simon & Schuster. '70.

Deming, Richard. Women: the new criminals. Nelson. '77.

*Editorial Research Reports on Crime and Justice. Congressional Quarterly. Washington, D.C. '78.
    Reprinted in this volume: Computer Crime. Marc Leepson. Editorial Research Reports. 1, no 1:3–13. Ja. 6, '78.

*Ianni, Francis A. J. Black mafia: ethnic succession in organized crime. Simon & Schuster. '74.

Lineberry, William P., ed. Justice in America: law, order, and the courts. (Reference Shelf. v 44, no 1) H. W. Wilson Company. '72.

Mitford, Jessica. Kind and usual punishment: the prison business. Knopf. '73.

Nelli, Humbert S. The business of crime: Italians and syndicate crime in the United States. Oxford University Press. '76.

Reid, Sue Titus. Crime and criminology, 2nd edition. Holt, Rinehart, and Winston. '79.

*Silberman, Charles E. Criminal violence, criminal justice. Random House. '78.

Steel, Ronald, ed. New light on juvenile delinquency. H. W. Wilson. '67.

*United States. Department of Justice. O. 18, '78. Press release issued by the Federal Bureau of Investigation. (1977 crime statistics) The Department. Washington, D.C. 20535. '78.

*United States. Department of Justice. Uniform crime reports for the United States, 1977. '78. The Department. Washington, D.C. 20535. '78.

*United States. President's Commission on Law Enforcement and Administration of Justice. The challenge of crime in a free society. Government Printing Office. Washington, D.C. '67.

Wilson, James Q. Thinking about crime. Basic Books. '75.
    Report reprinted in Avon Books ed. '68.

PERIODICALS

*Annals of the American Academy of Political and Social Science.
    423:1. Ja. '76. Crime and justice in America: 1776–1976; sym-
    posium, G. R. Newman, ed.
    Reprinted in this volume: Blacks, crime, and American cul-
    ture. John A. Davis. p 89–98; No excuse for crime. Ernest van
    den Haag. p 133–141.
Annals of the American Academy of Political and Social Science.
    434:114–36. N. '77. Contemporary crime in historical perspec-
    tive; a comparative study of London, Stockholm, and Sydney.
    T. R. Gurr
Annals of the American Academy of Political and Social Science.
    434: 137–50. N. '77. Sociological criminology and models of
    juvenile delinquency and maladjustment. Denis Szabo.
Business Week. p 66+. Je. 13, '77. War on white-collar crime.
*Business Week. p. 100–1+. F. 6, '78. Business buys the lie de-
    tector.
Car & Driver. 22:47–8+. Ap. '77. Steal-to-order biz: is your car
    next? K. Snedaker.
Center Magazine. 11:17. Ja. '78. Anomalies in prison sentences.
    C. B. Motley.
*Center Magazine. 11:74–9. Ja. '78. Criminal ethos. T. R. Gurr.
Clearing House. 51:58–9. O. '77. Ethnic comparison of juvenile
    offenses and socioeconomic status. George Calhoun, Jr.
*Commentary. 62:55–58. N. '76. Who is in prison? J. Q. Wilson.
Congressional Digest. 55:193–224. Ag. '76. This month's feature:
    the controversy over mandatory sentences.
Crawdaddy. p 32–8. F.'78. For a few dollars more; commercial
    crimes. Jim Hougan.
Crime and Delinquency. 23:41–50. Ja. '77. Dimensions of the dark
    figure of unreported crime. W. G. Skogan.
*Crime and Delinquency. 23:304–311. Jl. '77. Organized crime in
    the construction industry. R. C. Thomas, III.
Current History. 70:241–77. Je. '76. Criminal justice in America;
    symposium.
Current History. 71:1–36. Jl. '76. Reforming the criminal justice
    system; symposium.
*Daedalus. 107, no 1:143–157. Real and perceived changes of crime
    and punishment. M. E. Wolfgang.
Field & Stream. 81:72–3. Ja. '77. Gun laws: some work, some don't.
    E. B. Mann.
Forbes. 120:43–5+. D. 15, '77. Cigarette bootlegging: who says
    crime doesn't pay? James Cook.

Harper's Magazine. 255:16–20. N. '77. Changing criminal sentences. J. Q. Wilson.

Human Behavior. 7:58. S. '78. Crime wave that wasn't; study by Mark Fishman.

Human Behavior. 7:35. O. '78. Death row bias: white homicides are more prized than blacks; study by William Bowers.

Human Behavior. 8:36–7. F. '79. New link found: life stress can land a person in jail. Minuru Masuda.

Humanist. 38:16–19. S. '78. Criminal personality: new concepts and new procedures for change; study by Samuel Yochelson. S. E. Samenow.

Intellect. 103:312–14. F. '75. Convicted offenders' perception of the criminal justice process; Mansfield state reformatory study. P. C. Kratcoski and Kirk Scheuerman.

Intellect. 103:391–4. Mr. '75. Economics of punishing convicted misdemeanants. J. M. Rock and S. E. Reynolds.

Intellect. 104:98–102. S. '75. National strategy for crime prevention and control. C. R. Jeffery and I. A. Jeffery.

Intellect. 105:254–7. F. '77. Mobilizing eyewitnesses to crime: the use of radios and rewards. J. P. Levine.

Intellect. 106:11–12. Jl. '77. Increase of female criminals. R. D. Wright and S. E. Wright.

Intellect. 106:187. N. '77. Computer criminals; excerpt from address. D. B. Parker.

Intellect. 106:264. Ja. '78. Pros and cons of victimization surveys. J. P. Levine.

*Juris Doctor. 7:24+. My. '77. Liberal solution number 1,666,666. B. H. Wolfe.

Nation. 225:611–12. D. 10, '77. Dying institution; views of A. Amsterdam. Carey McWilliams.

National Review. 28:734–5. Jl. 9, '76. Crime and etiquette. S. S. McDonald.

National Review. 30:395–7+. Mr. 31, '78. Collapse of the case against capital punishment. Ernest van den Haag.

Nation's Business. 65:64–6. S. '77. Finding allies in the fight against shop-lifting. T. J. Housel.

*Nation's Cities. 16:16–18. S. '78. The victimizers. Lee Brown.

*Natural History. 85:16–18. Mr. '76. Criminal man revived; theories of Cesare Lombroso. S. J. Gould.

*New Republic. 166:17–21. Ap. 29, '72. Crime in the suites. Ralph Nader and Mark Green.

New Republic. 174:3–5. My. 1, '76. Of two minds about crime; question of minimum sentencing legislation.

*New York Daily News. p 3+. D. 13, '78. 2 losers at Brinksman-
  ship salute JFK caper. Pete Hamill.
New York Review of Books. 24:3–4+. Ja. 26, '78. Stir crazy.
  Clifford Geertz.
*New York Times. Sec. IV, p 6. S. 18, '77. Fuzzy crime statistics.
  Richard Lyons.
*New York Times. p 27 O. 26, '77. A prospect of less crime in the
  1980's. Jackson Toby.
*New York Times. Sec IV, p. 8. D. 18, '77. Causes of crime, maybe.
  Virginia Adams.
*New York Times. p 45. N. 7, '78. Justice. C. E. Silberman.
*New York Times. p 1+. D. 24, '78. Crime rising in south and
  west. W. K. Stevens.
New York Times Magazine. p 7+. D. 28, '75. Let the punishment
  fit the crime; indeterminate sentencing. A. M. Dershowitz.
New York Times Magazine. p 8–9+. Ja. 23, '77. Case against
  capital punishment. Abe Fortas.
New Yorker. p 35–8+. Ag. 22; 34–6+. Ag. 29, '77. Annals of
  crime. Thomas Whiteside.
Newsweek. 87:112. Ap. 12, '76. Death by friendly fire; failure of
  criminal rehabilitation, case of Kenny Dawson. Meg Green-
  field.
Newsweek. 88:26+. S. 6, '76. Breakdown; crime in People's Re-
  public of China.
Newsweek. 88:39. N. 29, '76. Crib jobs; crimes against the elderly.
  Richard Steele.
Newsweek. 90:101. O. 3, '77. Crime on the farm; rural property
  theft. J. K. Footlick and others.
Newsweek. 82:134. O. 23, '78. White fear, black crime; views of
  C. E. Silberman.
Outdoor Life. 161:12+. F. '78. Crime in the outdoors; preventive
  measures for visitors to the national parks. R. Starnes.
*Psychology Today. 9:42+. N. '75. The rise of the female crook.
  Freda Adler.
    Excerpted from Sisters in Crime. McGraw-Hill. '75.
Psychology Today. 9:110–111+. My. '76. Portrait of a mass killer.
  C. Campbell.
Psychology Today. 10:48–51+. O. '76. Who would kill a presi-
  dent? Little brother. I. Harris.
Psychology Today. 10:70–2+. Mr. '77. Justice for whom? plea
  bargaining. Steven Phillips.
Psychology Today. 10:98+. My. '77. Two answers: tough ordi-
  nances, tougher words. Jody Gaylin.
Psychology Today. 11:22+. Jl. '77. Making the punishment fix the
  crime; Law Enforcement Assistance Administration program.
  Debra Cohen.

Psychology Today. 11:34+. O. '77. Inalienable right to be robbed;
    comparison of Japanese and American crime prevention tech-
    niques. Jody Gaylin.
Psychology Today. 11:38. O. '77. United States, the most punitive
    nation; report of comparison study. Jody Gaylin.
Psychology Today. 11:96–7+. O. '77. Education of John Allen:
    excerpt from Assault with a deadly weapon: the autobiog-
    raphy of a street criminal, ed. by Philip Heymann and Dianne
    Kelly; with comment by Orde Coombs. John Allen.
Psychology Today. 11:68–70+. N. '77. Shy murderers. M. Lee and
    others.
Psychology Today. 11:33+. D. '77. New ways to spot serious crimi-
    nals early; study by Joan Petersilia and others. Debra Cohen.
Psychology Today. 11:86–7+. F. '78. Cold new look at the criminal
    mind; study by Samuel Yochelson and S. E. Samenow. M. S.
    Serrill.
Psychology Today. 11:35–6. Ap. '78. Behavioral approach to re-
    ducing recidivism; study by David Clement. Jack Horn.
*Public Interest. no 44:55–68. Summer '76. Learning about crime
    —the Japanese experience. D. H. Bayley.
Reader's Digest. 109:126–7. Ag. '76. Whoever steals, lives better;
    economic cheating of the state by Russians. C. S. Wren.
Reader's Digest. 109:109–17. D. '76. Case no H074–2092, homi-
    cide; tracking down a criminal. N. M. Adams.
Reader's Digest. 110:61–5. Je '77. Crime in America—a turnaround
    at last? E. H. Methvin.
Reader's Digest. 110:109–13. F. '77. I catch a burglar; Career
    Criminal Program. John Berendt.
Saturday Review. 5:10–13. Je. 10, '78. Getting away with murder:
    our disastrous court system. Nicholas Scoppetta.
*Saturday Review. 5:14–17. Je. 10, '78. Making things happen:
    the genius of Harold Rothwax. Loudon Wainwright.
Science. 199:665–8. F. 10, '78. Patuxent: controversial prison clings
    to belief in rehabilitation. C. Holden.
Science Digest. 84:65–7. S. '78. Women and violent behavior:
    natural cycle suspected as link in crime. T. O. Marsh.
Science News. 107:87–8. F. 8, '75. Science and law: the odd couple.
Scientific American. 237:56+. Jl. '77. How much crime?
Senior Scholastic. 109:18–19. Ap. 7. '77. Teenage criminals: time
    to get tough on toughs?
Society. 13:30–2. Mr. '76. Spontaneous vigilantes. R. L. Shotland.
Society. 13:38–43. Mr. '76. Community self-defense. G. T. Marx
    and Dane Archer.
Sports Illustrated. 48:62–6+. F. 6, '78. Stealing was my specialty;
    excerpt from Breakout, ed. by Jim Hawkins. Ron LeFlore.
Time. 107:82–4. Ap. 26. '76. Crime and punishment. Bicentennial

essay. J. Q. Wilson.

*Time. 110:18–20+. Je. 11, '77. The youth crime plague.

*Time. 110:59–60. S. 26, '77. The pinch must really sting; study by the Institute for Law and Social Research.

Time. 110:98–9. D. 12. '77. Fixed sentences gain favor.

Time. 111:62. Ja. 30, '78. Stopping crime as a career; Major Violators Program.

U.S. News & World Report. 79:21–5. Ag. 25, '75. Big change in prisons: punish—not reform.

U.S. News & World Report. 80:50–2. F. 9, '76. Crime's big payoff; how much do successful criminals make?

U.S. News & World Report. 81:80–2. N. 15, '76. Behind the trend to go easy on victimless crimes.

U.S. News & World Report. 81:73–5. N. 22, '76. War on career criminals starts to show results.

*U.S. News & World Report. 82:47–8. F. 21, '77. A $40-billion crime wave swamps American business.

U.S. News & World Report. 82:57–8. F. 28, '77. Why violent crime is now in fashion; interview, F. J. Hacker.

*U.S. News & World Report. 82:82. Ap. 11, '77. Why government alone can't end the crime wave. G. M. Caplan.

U.S. News & World Report. 82:33–4. My. 2, '77. Now it's Russia that fights a crime wave.

U.S. News & World Report. 82:61–3. Je. 20, '77. From an expert —some ideas on what's needed to fight crime; interview. Norval Morris.

U.S. News & World Report. 83:47–8. S. 5, '77. Stepped-up drive to make punishment fit the crime.

U.S. News & World Report. 83:89–90. O. 10, '77. As crime in the U.S. starts to level off—.

U.S. News & World Report. 84:45–6. Ja. 30, '78. Outlaw lie-detector tests?; interviews with Birch Bayh and Ty Kelley.

U.S. News & World Report. 86:52–4. Ja. 20, '79. As FBI charts a new course—its main targets now; interview with William H. Webster.

Vital Speeches. 42:524–30. Je. 15. '76. Building new support for enforcing the law; public attitudes on crime and law enforcement; address, May 9, 1976. Philip Lesly.

Vital Speeches. 42:731–3. S. 15, '76. Making our criminal justice system work; address, May 24, 1976. Dan Walker.

Vital Speeches. 43:525–7. Je. 15, '77. White collar crime; address, May 9, 1977. H. E. Groves.

*Washington Post. p C5. N. 20, '77. A 'criminal personality'? Patrick Young.